WHAT'S THE DIFFERENCE?

WHAT'S THE DIFFERENCE?

Recreational Culinary
Reference for the
Curious and Confused

BRETTE WARSHAW

HARPER WAVE

An Imprint of HarperCollins*Publishers*

Illustrations by Sophia Foster-Dimino

WHAT'S THE DIFFERENCE? Copyright © 2021 by Brette Warshaw.
All rights reserved. Printed in Canada.
No part of this book may be used or reproduced in any
manner whatsoever without written permission except in
the case of brief quotations embodied in critical articles
and reviews. For information, address HarperCollins
Publishers, 195 Broadway, New York, NY 10007.

HarperCollins books may be purchased for
educational, business, or sales promotional use.
For information, please email the Special Markets
Department at SPsales@harpercollins.com.

FIRST EDITION

Designed by Leah Carlson-Stanisic

Library of Congress Cataloging-in-
Publication Data has been applied for.

ISBN 978-0-06-299619-0

21 22 23 24 25   TC   10 9 8 7 6 5 4 3 2 1

For J

Contents

Cheese

Chocolate

Coffee

Introduction

We all like to feel smart. Sometimes, that means muscling through *On the Origin of Species* or Plato's *Republic*. Other times, that means reading a few hundred words about the slight differences between quotidian things—like seltzer and club soda, or jam and jelly, or sweet potatoes and yams—and becoming incrementally more knowledgeable, arming yourself with the kind of information that makes the world a little more interesting.

I launched the *What's the Difference?* newsletter in February 2018 to fill that need. The premise was simple: once a week, I would write about the difference between things that were confused for one another. I polled a few friends, started a spreadsheet with future topics, and got to work. Week after week, the audience grew, and so did that spreadsheet; people wrote in with their own ideas, and the newsletter became something we all built together.

What you have in your hands now is the very best of the food-and-drink category: the product of years of research, interviews, and, well, eating. Whether you're a chef, a passionate home cook, or someone who would drink Soylent for every meal and be absolutely thrilled about it, I bet you'll learn something new. I know I did while writing it.

Active Dry Yeast vs. Fresh Yeast vs. Instant Yeast

When we bake bread—or croissants, or cinnamon rolls, or pizza, or pretzels—we are at the mercy of a puny, ancient, single-celled organism: *Saccharomyces cerevisiae*, also known as yeast. It's a humbling experience, really: if you've ever had to try to convince yourself that the leaden, insulator-foam-textured focaccia you just made isn't really *that bad* while staring at the fluffy, ethereal versions on the internet, you've gotten a sense of how much work that tiny creature can do.

The first step to getting yeast to work for you is to use the right type. The three options: fresh, active dry, and instant. **Fresh yeast** is light, soft, and extremely perishable; it needs to be kept in the fridge and only lasts a few weeks. It's 70 percent water by weight, and 100 percent of the yeast cells are living and active. That means that it needs no proofing you can crumble it right into the recipe. As for the flavor: while all yeast tastes, well, yeasty, fresh yeast is decidedly more so. "It's a little more floral, a little more noticeable," says baking expert and cookbook author Erin McDowell. "If you gave me three things made with the three kinds of yeast, I'd be able to pick out the one that's fresh."

Active dry yeast is granulated and sold in glass jars or individual quarter-ounce packets. To make the product—which is 95 percent dry matter—the yeast gets exposed to such high temperatures that many of the cells are destroyed. That means that it needs to be "proofed" (dissolved in a warm liquid, ideally between 105 and 115°F) before getting used in a recipe. The liquid sloughs off the dead cells and exposes the active, living ones, which start happily making bubbles when they're ready to go.

Instant yeast, like active dry yeast, is granulated and made of 95 percent dry matter—but the drying process is gentler, which means all of those dried particles are active. It therefore doesn't need to be proofed and can be added straight into a recipe. Instant yeast also works quicker than active dry yeast, with a rise time that's approximately 50 percent speedier. That, plus eliminating the minutes spent staring at your proofing liquid trying to decide if there are actually bubbles or not, can save you some time in the kitchen.

Now, for the big question: Can you substitute one type of yeast for the other? Kind of. McDowell recommends keeping fresh yeast in its own category, and only swapping it in for the granulated stuff if you really know what you're doing. But if you have instant yeast and need active dry, according to *Modernist Bread* author Nathan Myhrvold, you can multiply the amount by 1.33; if you have active dry yeast but need instant yeast, multiply it by 0.75.

Aioli vs. Mayonnaise

At some point in the American collective conscience, mayonnaise got pushed aside for aioli: its sexy, foreign counterpart that made every sandwich sound instantly more gourmet. People started going around saying, "I don't like mayo, but I *love* aioli." What's the deal? Are they actually that different?

Both mayonnaise and aioli are emulsions: a mixture of two or more liquids that really don't like each other. Think oil and water, or oil and any water-based substance. In order for the two things to emulsify, the oil needs to be broken down into teeny-tiny droplets, which then get suspended in the mixture. The result: a thick concoction with a texture altogether different from the two liquids on their own.

In the case of **mayonnaise**, oil is mixed with egg yolk, salt, and an acid like lemon juice or vinegar. Sometimes there's mustard in there too, to help things along. The result: a thick, velvety, pleasantly bland condiment.

Classic **aioli**, which can be found in Spain and other Mediterranean cuisines, is just a mixture of oil, garlic, and **salt**, whipped into a creamy, potent spread. No egg yolk, no mustard. But these days, "aioli" is used to describe any kind of flavored mayo—whether it's spiked with garlic, chipotle, pesto, paprika ... you name it. It's just mayo with stuff in it.

So to all the folks out there who lather up their sandwiches with truffle aioli ... sorry babe, you're just eating mayo.

All-Purpose Flour vs. Bread Flour vs. Cake Flour vs. Pastry Flour

Remember in the beginning of the coronavirus pandemic, when you couldn't find a bag of all-purpose flour at even the most random of grocery stores? I bet you were wondering if that old bag of cake flour in the back of your pantry could feed your sourdough hobby, or if you could use bread flour to try your hand at homemade pasta. That's the problem with flours being labeled by their specific use: it's great if you're baking bread or cake or pastry, but not if you're attempting any off-the-cuff decisions.

All-purpose, bread, pastry, and cake flours are all white flours, which means the wheat grains (also known as wheat-berries) have been stripped of their bran and germ, leaving just the starchy endosperm. What makes them different from one another—and particularly good for their label-sanctioned uses—is their protein content. Flour contains two types of protein: glutenin, which makes the dough elastic, and gliadin, which gives the dough the ability to stretch to get a higher rise. The more protein, the chewier and firmer your final product will be; with less protein, you'll get a delicate, finer crumb.

Here are the most common types of flour and what each of them is good for.

All-Purpose Flour

All-purpose flour is true to its name: it's strong enough for breads and light enough for baked goods, making it the ultimate pantry workhorse. Look for an unbleached variety, which means that it hasn't been chemically treated to whiten it.

(When flour is first milled, it has a yellowish color, which fades to white as it ages.) The protein content of all-purpose flour actually varies across the country: U.S. national brands have 11–12 percent, while regional brands in the South and Pacific Northwest have 7.5–9.5 percent. If you're looking for a consistent final product, it's best to stick to the national brands— that's what most recipes are written for. (Unless you're making biscuits, in which case you'd want to track down White Lily.)

Bread Flour

Bread flour has a protein content of 12–13 percent, making it great for things like bagels, country loaves, and certain types of pizza. (And yes, you can use it for your sourdough.) For softer breads like white bread or challah or dinner rolls, you'll probably want to stick with AP.

Pastry Flour

With its protein content of 8–9 percent, pastry flour is great for making tender baked goods with a fine, delicate crumb. Think quick breads, muffins, and certain types of cookies.

Cake Flour

Is cake a pastry? Yes. But cake flour is different from pastry flour: It has a lower protein content (7–8 percent) and is treated with chlorine dioxide or chlorine gas, which makes the proteins even weaker. The chemicals also affect the flour's starch granules, giving them the ability to carry more weight and allowing you to incorporate more sugar and liquid into a dough than you'd otherwise be able to. Though many cake recipes call for all-purpose flour, things with a particularly airy crumb, like angel food cake, rely on cake flour for texture.

Aperol vs. Campari vs. Cynar

Aperol, Campari, and Cynar are all Italian *aperitivi*: light alcoholic drinks meant to be sipped before a meal to rev up the appetite. They're also all *amari*: liqueurs (page 143) made bitter with spices, herbs, and roots. Many amari have over thirty of those botanical ingredients, things like gentian and wormwood and angelica root and other spooky-sounding items that sound like they belong in a witches' brew.

The history of amari dates back to the medieval times, when monks would use local botanicals to make medicinal elixirs. The liqueurs themselves started emerging in the nineteenth century, and by the 1920s, they were considered so Italian that drinking them was "practically an act of patriotism," writes cookbook author Katie Parla in *Punch*. Up until the 1980s, amari were distinctly regional; your favorite amaro probably depended on the area you came from. Now they're big business, so much so that Gruppo Campari actually owns Aperol, Campari, and Cynar, among others.

Aperitivo liqueurs can be divided into two categories: "aperitivo" (yes, confusing) and "bitter." "Aperitivo" drinks are sweeter than the "bitter" ones and contain around half as much alcohol. **Aperol** is the most well-known "aperitivo"; you've likely had it in an Aperol spritz. It's a red-orange color and includes sweet and bitter oranges, rhubarb, gentian, and cinchona bark, giving it a distinctly fruity flavor with a bitter, herbal edge. Its ABV (alcohol by volume) is 11 percent, the lowest of the group.

Campari is the most well-known liqueur in the "bitter" category, famous for its role in the classic negroni. Until 2006, its

unmissable bright-red hue came from dye made of the dried, pulverized bodies of the cochineal, a small insect. (Now, it comes from artificial colors.) Campari is significantly more intense than aperol, both in bitterness and alcohol content; its ABV ranges from 20.5 to 28 percent, depending on where it's sold. It's made with oranges, rhubarb, ginseng, and "herbs"—though the type of herbs is unclear. The only official ingredients that the company will disclose are alcohol and water.

Cynar, pronounced "chee-NAR," is a dark brown amaro with an ABV of 16.5 percent. It's infused with artichokes—"Cynar" comes from the vegetable's Latin name, *Cynara scolymus*—along with twelve undisclosed herbs. The result: a bitter, slightly vegetal liqueur, with a caramelly sweetness that makes it surprisingly pleasant to drink. Try swapping it in for Campari in your next negroni, and you may never look back.

Appetizers vs. Canapés vs. Hors d'Oeuvres

Throwing a fancy cocktail party this weekend? Serving up trays of canapés to your Champagne-sipping comrades? There's no better way to de-class the situation than by calling your finger foods by the wrong name, so read up.

Appetizer is the most general term and refers to anything served before a main course (page 124) to whet the appetite. That could mean those finger foods you're passing around, or a salad course, or even some bowls of chips and dip.

Hors d'oeuvres are specifically one- or two-bite foods, either hot or cold, served with aperitivi (page 6) or cocktails. A crudités platter counts as an hors d'oeuvre, as do pigs in a blanket.

A **canapé** is a type of hors d'oeuvre composed of a small piece of bread, cracker, or pastry crowned with some sort of topping: cheese, meat, tinned fish, etc. The term comes from the French word for "couch"—maybe because the bread/cracker is a couch for the stuff on top of it, or because the best way to consume them is while being propped up by cushions? That's for you to decide.

How Many Hors d'Oeuvres Do You Need for a Party?

According to Martha Stewart's book *Entertaining*: If you're throwing a cocktail party with no seated dinner, plan for eight different hors d'oeuvres with three of each per guest. But if they involve shrimp or caviar, Martha says, "I further augment the portion per person, because such expensive treats bring out everyone's gastronomic zeal." Well said, Martha!

Apple Cider vs. Apple Juice

To make **apple cider**, apples are cored, chopped, mashed, and then pressed to extract their liquid. The result is a cloudy, caramel-colored elixir that tastes of brisk fall mornings and flannel shirts and scratchy-butted hayrides. Most cider is pasteurized before being sold, but you can sometimes find unpasteurized stuff at a local orchard or farmers' market.

With **apple juice**, apples go through the same process as apple cider, but the liquid is then filtered to remove any pulp and sediment. The result is pasteurized, mixed with potassium sorbate (a preservative) to prevent fermentation, and sometimes sweetened with sugar or corn syrup. The filtration process removes some of the apples' nuance—those tart, husky, bassnotey flavors you'll taste in cider—and makes the liquid lighter in color and more clear. This is what fills kids' juice boxes and pairs wonderfully with animal crackers.

Seems simple, right? There's a catch: the United States has no national legal definition for either product, which means that in many states, apple cider and apple juice can technically be the same thing. Martinelli's, whose sparkling cider you've likely had at a corporate holiday celebration or baby shower, even admits on their own website that the only difference between their juice and cider is the label.

And all bets are off in Europe, where "cider" refers to the bubbly, fermented, alcoholic liquid we think of as "hard cider" in the U.S.—not exactly what you want to send with your kid's lunch.

Apple Butter vs. Applesauce

Both **applesauce** and **apple butter** are made by cooking down apples with water, spices, and sometimes a bit of sugar. The difference between them? Time. **Applesauce** spends less time on the stove (or in the oven), which means it's looser and lighter colored. It can be smooth or chunky, depending on how much of it is pureed.

Keep cooking down applesauce, and you'll eventually get **apple butter**, a thick, caramelized spread. The only thing it has in common with actual butter is its texture; in fact, it has more of a kinship with the spreads/preserves/compote family (page 96) than anything dairy. Serve it on toast or waffles, use it on a sandwich, or swirl it into a bowl of yogurt or oatmeal.

Arepa vs. Gordita
vs. Pupusa

Arepas are to Colombian and Venezuelan cuisine as tortillas are to Mexico and bread is to France: something consumed at breakfast, lunch, dinner, and everything in between. They are traditionally made by soaking and pounding dried corn in a *pilón*, a large mortar and pestle—but these days, most people just use precooked, dehydrated cornmeal, known as arepa flour and sold as *masarepa*. The arepa flour gets mixed with water, salt, and sometimes butter and/or grated cheese; the dough is then shaped into cakes and baked, grilled, steamed, or fried. Once cooked, the arepas can be sliced open and filled with ingredients—such as beans, cheese, meat, eggs, vegetables, or seafood—left whole and garnished with toppings, or simply eaten on their own, maybe with butter and salt.

Farther north, in El Salvador, you'll find **pupusas**: thick corn cakes filled with cheese, a finely ground pork mixture called *chicharrón*, refried beans, and/or loroco, a flower. Unlike arepas, pupusas are made with instant masa, *masa harina*, which is mixed with warm water to form a dough. The fillings are then cooked *into* the cake, which gets griddled on a *comal*, making for a tidy, self-contained final product—maybe with a tiny lace-edging of barely escaped cheese. The finished pupusas are served with a spicy, lightly fermented cabbage slaw called *curtido* and a loose tomato salsa.

We finish our corn-cake tour in Mexico, land of the **gordita**. Spanish for "little fat one," gorditas are like chubby corn tortillas, made with masa or masa harina and shaped around a quarter- to a half-inch thick. They're fried, griddled, or a combination of the two, then sliced open and filled with things like refried beans and cheese, stewed pork, chorizo and eggs, or *picadillo*, a mixture of ground beef and potatoes. And since gorditas are sturdier than tortillas, they're particularly good at cradling their contents: a leak-safe pocket you can eat on the go.

Armagnac vs. Cognac

Both Cognac and Armagnac are types of brandy: a spirit made from fermented fruit juice. That fermented juice can come from grapes (for wine), apples (for calvados), tree fruit (for schnapps), or a number of other earthly delights. In the case of Cognac and Armagnac, we're dealing with products made from wine.

Where They're From

Cognac is from Cognac, and Armagnac is from Armagnac, a pleasingly straightforward differentiation. Both are regions in Western France; Cognac bumps up against the Atlantic Ocean, while Armagnac, around 150 miles to the southeast, is landlocked.

What They're Made From

"Both Cognac and Armagnac are made from a shockingly undrinkable wine," says writer Aliza Kellerman on *VinePair*. Cognac is only made from the Ugni Blanc grape, while Armagnac uses three more: Folle Blanche, Colombard, and Baco Blanc.

How They're Made

Cognac goes through two rounds of distillation in a pot still, while Armagnac only goes through one round in a column still. (For more information about stills, see page 143.) Armagnac comes off the still at around 52–60 percent ABV, and unless it's blended or bottled at cask strength, it gets diluted to around 45–47 percent. Cognac comes off the still at around 70 percent ABV and is bottled at 40 percent.

How They're Aged

Though the grapes, terroir, and distillation style are all important, "for the most part, these spirits get their character from long barrel-aging," says Jim Meehan, author of *Meehan's Bartender Manual.* Cognac usually hangs out in oak barrels made of trees from the Limousin or Tronçais forests. Armagnac is usually aged in local Monlezun black oak, which imparts more flavor than the Cognac barrels and allows for a faster aging process. Both brandies are sold either as vintages, which come from a single year, or blends, in which producers blend young specimens with small amounts of older ones.

What They Taste Like

Cognac is usually softer and rounder than Armagnac; since Armagnac is only distilled once, it can be fuller, more complex, and a bit brasher. In *Drink What You Want*, John deBary recommends trying out Armagnac as a whiskey substitute in a cocktail.

How They're Labeled

For Cognac:

V.S. ("Very special"): the youngest brandy in the blend is aged at least two years

V.S.O.P. ("Very superior old pale"): aged at least four years

Napoleon: aged at least six years

X.O. ("Extra old"): aged at least ten years

For Armagnac:

V.S.: the youngest brandy in the blend is aged at least one year

V.S.O.P.: aged at least four years

X.O.: aged at least ten years

How to smell and taste Armagnac

In researching this topic, I came across many flowery descriptions of how best to fully experience a high-quality Armagnac. Please enjoy this excerpt from an old *New York* magazine wine guide:

> Appreciating the bouquet is the first critical step in the enjoyment of this most beguiling libation. . . . Hold the glass at chest level and let the delicate fragrances waft up. In a minute or so, your senses will be luxuriating in a cloud of vanilla, toffee, nougat, pepper, rose, and chocolate. . . .
>
> Stick a finger in the glass and then dab the liquid on the back of your hand—just as you would a perfume sample. Your body heat will cause the alcohol to evaporate, leaving behind only the essential aromas of the Armagnac. After about a minute, smell it up close. The Armagnac will no doubt remind you of dried fruits like apricots, prunes, and figs, and you may also detect butterscotch, licorice, and flowers.
>
> Now take the tiniest sip of the Armagnac—about a half-teaspoonful. Roll the liquid around your tongue, your cheeks, and your gums. Drinking it this way, you'll see why people love this stuff.

Baking vs. Roasting

Some words, like humans or national politics or a fine, aged Bordeaux, are nuanced. Some love to defy any clear definition and insist on getting treated like the very unique, darling snowflakes that they are. "Baking" and "roasting" are two such words. Here are some generalizations one could make about them, and all the ways they prove us wrong.

Generalization #1: Baking is for lower temperatures, and roasting is for higher temperatures.

Sure—you could hear this and nod and move on with your life, but you'd be missing half the picture. Baking is generally considered to happen below 350°F, with roasting at above 350°F. But this doesn't take into account the things that happen *at* 350°F—which are many. And some things that you'd consider "baking"—like cooking a pie crust—happen around 425°F, which is definitely above 350°F. You can also "slow-roast" fattier proteins like salmon between 200°F and 300°F, a technique that yields a very delicious, if not semantically maddening, result.

Generalization #2: Baking is for pastries, breads, and casseroles, and roasting is for meats and vegetables.

Have you ever heard of a baked potato?

Generalization #3: Baking is for making unstructured things more structured (cookie dough, cake batter, etc.), and roasting is for making structured things (chickens, carrots, prime rib) less structured.

Again: Have you ever heard of a baked potato?

Generalization #4: Roasting is always done in an uncovered pan, while baking happens in a covered pan.

I've baked one million cakes and cookies and pans of brownies in my life and I have never once covered the pan. Also, there's a certain point on Thanksgiving where the turkey looks done but isn't done so we cover it in aluminum foil to keep it from getting too brown. Does that mean we "bake" our Thanksgiving turkey? I don't think so.

Generalization #5: Roasting involves coating things in a layer of fat before cooking them, whereas baking does not.

This is a weird one, but I read it somewhere, so I have to acknowledge it. Sure, you don't toss balls of cookie dough or a pan of cake batter in olive oil before putting them in the oven. But if you decided to cook a whole chicken or a sheet pan of broccoli dry, they might burn and be not as delicious, but would that make them "baked?" Nope.

Baking Powder vs. Baking Soda

There are a number of situations in this book where the difference between certain things is slight, or negligible, or even nonexistent. This is not one of those situations. Baking soda and baking powder, in fact, are two very different things, and substituting one for the other would very likely ruin whatever you're cooking.

They do, however, rely on the same science. When you combine certain acids with certain alkaline ingredients, you get a reaction. One of the products of this reaction is carbon dioxide, the gas that makes things bubble and rise. Baking soda and baking powder leaven things by facilitating that reaction, though they do it in different ways.

Baking soda is the household name for sodium bicarbonate, or $NaHCO_3$. Sodium bicarbonate is an alkaline compound. In order to make something rise, it needs an acid to react with—think buttermilk, yogurt, brown sugar, chocolate, fruit juice, or non-Dutched cocoa powder (see page 91). Without enough acid in the mixture, the sodium bicarbonate would just stay sodium bicarbonate—and whatever you're baking would have a bitter, soapy, astringent aftertaste.

Baking powder, on the other hand, is a complete leavening system; it contains both alkaline baking soda and a solid, crystallized acid, usually cream of tartar. All it needs is some moisture, and the chemical reactions start popping off. Most supermarket baking powders are double-acting: They release an initial set of bubbles once they're added to the batter, and then another set during the baking process. (That is, unless you have a special baking powder made especially for restaurants or manufacturing, which contains slow-releasing acids that allow for more timing flexibility.)

So if it's as simple as BYO-acid versus I'm-a-strong-independent-pantry-item-and-I-can-leaven-things-on-my-own, why might a recipe call for both baking soda *and* baking powder? Recipes vary greatly in the amount of acid they have and in the taste and texture they're looking to achieve. Maybe there's not enough acid in the mix to fully leaven the dish, and it needs some extra powdered oomph. Maybe you actually *want* some acidic twang—think buttermilk biscuits or lemon tea cake—and don't want it all getting turned into bubbles. Baking soda and baking powder work in tandem to help you get there: to balance out the texture and flavor of the final dish, so you can have your cake and eat it, too.

Banana vs. Plantain

Bananas are the seedless berries (!) of a tree-sized herb (!) called *Musa sapientum*, which can grow up to twenty feet high. The species originated in Southeast Asia and is now grown in more than 150 countries. A plant produces one to twenty fruit clusters, also known as "hands," which each contain around ten to twenty individual pieces of fruit.

There are two major categories of bananas: **"dessert bananas,"** what we think of as simply "bananas" in the United States, and **plantains.** The major difference? Starch. All bananas store their energy as starch, some of which gets converted into sugar during the ripening process. In dessert bananas, that process is jacked up: a starch-to-sugar ratio of 25:1 transforms into a 1:20 ratio when the fruit is ripe. A lot less of plantains' starch gets converted into sugar; a ripe plantain is only 6 percent sugar, compared to a dessert banana's nearly 20 percent.

So what does that mean when it comes to the eating experience? Dessert bananas are soft and sweet, while plantains are drier and, well, starchier. While you probably peel and eat a banana without giving it a second thought, you'd almost never eat a plantain raw: the fruit is far better suited to cooking, whether it's ripe or not.

The dessert bananas you get at the grocery store in the U.S. are all a type called the Cavendish, by far the most common variety imported to non-tropical countries. But plantain varieties actually make up 85 percent of all global banana cultivation. They're a staple of many cuisines around the world:

sliced into coins and fried, fried and smashed and fried again, braised in broth, used in soup, and much, much more.

Some more fun facts about bananas and plantains:

- The name of the species, *Musa sapientum,* means "fruit of the wise men" and comes from a myth that Indian gurus would sit in the shade of the plants while they meditated.

- Though a few varieties dominate international trade, you can find bananas in all shapes, sizes, colors, and flavors at specialty markets: look for Blue Java (or Ice Cream) bananas, which have silvery-blue skin and taste like ice cream; Manzano bananas, which have a distinct strawberry-apple flavor; and Lady Finger bananas, which are three to four inches long and even sweeter than the Cavendish.

- Bananas go through a unique process called negative geotropism: They start growing towards the ground, then curl upwards, against gravity, towards the sun. This allows them to get as much light as possible without destabilizing the plant—and it's why they're curved!

- Because of the way they're propagated, banana varieties are especially vulnerable to disease and pests. A prime example: Until the 1950s, the Gros Michel banana, which is richer and sweeter than the type we eat now, dominated the international market. When the variety fell prey to a soil fungus, farmers were forced to abandon it altogether and start producing the Cavendish—which was immune to the specific disease that befell the Gros Michel—instead. Many scientists worry that the Cavendish, too, will one day go extinct.

Alabama vs. Kansas City vs. Kentucky vs. North Carolina vs. South Carolina vs. Texas Barbecue Sauces

These days, you'd be forgiven if you thought of barbecue sauce as the stuff that's next to ketchup at the supermarket, or what you dip McNuggets into when you're feeling frisky. But start traveling around the country and you'll find that the condiment is a regional phenomenon, deeply connected to the history of a place and its people. It's yellow and drizzle-able; it's clear and swirling with red-pepper-flake confetti; it's black and red and even creamy-white. Here's a snapshot of seven distinct Southern sauces.

Kansas City Barbecue Sauce

This is the style that dominates the American collective conscience: thick, red, spiced and sweet, heavy on the ketchup. According to barbecue expert Meathead Goldwyn, its complexity comes from multiple sources of sweetness (tomato paste or ketchup, brown sugar, molasses, honey), tartness (lemon juice, vinegar, steak sauce), and heat (chili powder, black pepper, mustard, hot sauce) along with garlic, onion, Worcestershire sauce, cumin, and salt. It also often has the addition of liquid smoke, which gives it what we think of as a "barbecue" flavor. Eat it on pork ribs—a specialty of the Kansas City area—and on meatloaf.

East Carolina Mop Sauce

East Carolina mop sauce is found on the coast of North and South Carolina, also known as the Low Country. It comes from the original pioneers of barbecue: the African slaves of Scottish settlers, who sauced their meat with a combination of vinegar, black pepper, and red pepper flakes. The mixture is used as a "mop" to baste the meat with while cooking as well as an accompaniment to the final dish. Unlike Kansas City sauce, it's meant to penetrate the meat, not just sit on top of it looking pretty. It lends magic to fatty foods like whole-hog barbecue, since the vinegar and spice cut through the meat.

Lexington Dip

Lexington dip hails from Lexington, North Carolina and the surrounding area. It's similar to East Carolina mop sauce but has a bit of ketchup or tomato paste in the mix, which adds a hint of sweetness. According to Goldwyn, it's great on pork, chicken, or turkey.

South Carolina Mustard Sauce

German immigrants in South Carolina knew the combo of pork and mustard was a winner, and they applied this wisdom to the barbecue of the region. The result: a sharp, slightly spicy sauce made with yellow mustard (page 117), vinegar, sugar, and spices, great on anything that comes off a pig.

Texas Mop Sauce

Texas mop sauce is a thin concoction made with vinegar, chili powder, cumin, hot sauce, onion, and a touch of ketchup. Pitmasters use it as a mop while cooking and as an accompaniment to the finished product. Many sauces in Texas actually have the addition of beef drippings or trimmings, which means they can't be bottled; Goldwyn describes sauce at the famous Cooper's in Llano as "a thin tomato soup with a beef-stock base." Unsurprisingly, it's great on the classic Texas barbecue dishes: beef ribs and brisket.

Alabama White Sauce

Over in Alabama, barbecue sauce is white: it's made with mayonnaise, vinegar, and various seasonings, such as garlic powder and mustard powder. Credit for the original recipe goes to Bob Gibson of Big Bob Gibson Bar-B-Q in Decatur, who started serving barbecue in 1925. While it's not great on pork—too much fat! it's transcendent on chicken and turkey.

Kentucky Black Barbecue Sauce

The most elusive of the bunch, black barbecue sauce can only be found in restaurants in western Kentucky, around the town of Owensboro. Made with white vinegar and Worcestershire sauce, it's featured in the specialty dish of the region: smoked mutton shoulder (page 141). Cooks use it as both a mop and a finishing sauce, but Goldwyn doesn't recommend trying it on its own—it's a far cry from the sweet-tangy stuff we're used to.

Barbecue vs. Grilling

What makes us human? Some scientists think that cooking—specifically, the use of fire to transform food from raw into cooked—is what separated *Homo erectus*, the first modern human species, from similar-sized primates. Heating food unlocked its nutrition and made it easier to eat, allowing our ancestors to spend less time searching for food and more time to do things other than chewing. The very act of cooking doubled our brain size over the course of 600,000 years.

And while these ancestors weren't charring up burgers and 'dogs, what they were doing could be called **barbecuing**. "Ultimately, it is smoke that differentiates barbecue from other types of cooking," says cookbook author Meathead Goldwyn. "There are many forms of barbecue around the world, and it is the presence of smoke that unifies them all."

Grilling, then, is a subset of barbecue. It involves direct heat from charcoal or a fire, coming from one direction; the heat is then transferred to the food by means of conduction, like when you put a chicken thigh on a grill grate and it starts to sizzle. That surface is usually 500°F to 800°F, which means that whatever you're grilling gets cooked quickly—and probably gets some char on it, too. Grilling therefore lends itself well to small, relatively tender cuts of meat—think steaks, chicken parts, hamburgers, and chops—as well as seafood, vegetables, and fruit.

So where do the briskets and the ribs and the pork butts—the stuff we think of in the U.S. as "barbecue"—fit in? That's **Southern barbecue**, and in fact, it's quite different from grilling. Rather than relying on ripping-hot heat, Southern barbecue is all about taking things low and slow. The coals and flames are set off to the side or far below the food, and the lid of the grill or smoker is kept closed; the heat is then transferred through convection, in which the heat and smoke circulate and commingle around whatever's being cooked. The temperatures for Southern barbecue are usually in the 200°F to 300°F range, making the cooking process a much slower ride—especially since the technique is used for larger, tougher cuts of meat, such as brisket, ribs, pork shoulders (page 173), and even whole animals. The process allows for the connective tissue to properly break down, resulting in that transcendent fall-apart texture that people stay up all night tending fire (or just waiting in really long lines) for.

And how about the spelling—is it barbecue, barbeque, BBQ, B-B-Que, Bar-B-Q, Bar-B-Que, Bar-B-Cue, or some other permutation? Because the word originally comes from *barbacoa*—the Spanish interpretation of a word used by the Taino tribe in the Caribbean—linguists and historians generally agree that the correct term is "barbecue."

Beefsteak vs. Cherry vs. Grape vs. Heirloom vs. Plum Tomatoes

Let's first take a slight detour from our guiding question to ask another one: Why are grocery-store tomatoes so bad?

There are two major categories of tomatoes: **heirlooms**, which we'll cover below, and **hybrids**. The tomatoes you'll find year-round in the grocery store are hybrids, which means that humans have cultivated and bred them for specific character-istics. Not all hybrids are bad, but the grocery-store ones are; they're bred for resistance to diseases, firm flesh, thick skin, and storage potential, rather than, say, flavor. They're also yanked from their plants while they're still hard as rocks so that they don't get crushed on the way to their final destina-tion. Off the vine, they can't develop the sugars and acids and other flavor/aroma chemicals that make them actually taste good—so they're sprayed with ethylene gas instead, which induces reddening and softening. The result: watery, cottony pucks.

Heirloom tomatoes are "open-pollinated," which means the varietal comes from natural pollination (birds, insects, wind, etc.) rather than scientists. These types of tomatoes "breed true," which means that if you plant one of its seeds, it will grow into a plant that bears tomatoes that look just like the parent. (Hybrids, on the other hand, will give birth to plants that exhibit different characteristics from each of the parents; it takes around seven generations for cultivars to stabilize.) Heirlooms come from plants that have been grown without

Heirloom

Beefsteak

Plum

Cherry

Grape

Cocktail

crossbreeding for at least fifty years. They're found in all different colors, shapes, and sizes: perfectly oval; craggy and bulbous; heart-shaped; yellow, green, black, pink, striped, tie-dye. Their names are just as varied: Black Krim, Mr. Stripey, Green Zebra, Brandywine, Cherokee Purple. These are the guys you'll find at the farmers' market at the peak of the season, the ones that just beg to be sliced and salted and eaten pretty much as is.

Beefsteak tomatoes are notable for their size—they can weigh in at over a pound each, with a diameter of six or more inches—and their texture: they have smaller seed cavities than other types of tomatoes, giving them a greater ratio of flesh to juice and seeds. There are around 350 types of beefsteaks out there, and they can be either heirloom or hybrid. And although you'll mainly see the red ones labeled as "beefsteaks," they can come in all colors: pink, yellow, green, white, technicolor. The Brandywine, Cherokee Purple, and Black Krim heirlooms, for example, are all beefsteak tomatoes, too.

Plum tomatoes, also known as Roma or paste tomatoes, are oval-shaped and smaller than beefsteaks. They also have a lower water content compared to other types, with an almost chewy flesh—making them particularly suited to sauce-making. These are the tomatoes you'll see everywhere in Italy, the most famous type being the San Marzano.

And let's not forget the baby tomatoes: the cherries, grapes, and cocktails. **Cherry tomatoes** are the small, round guys with thin skins that squirt juice everywhere when you bite into them. They're super sweet and have a high water content, and they come in many colors.

Grape tomatoes are the oblong, grape-shaped ones that you'll often find in the grocery store; they have a lower water content and thicker skins than cherry tomatoes, which help them last longer.

Cocktail tomatoes are larger than grape and cherry tomatoes but still of the small, sweet ilk. They're grown hydroponically and can be found in many grocery stores. If you're looking for a decent specimen outside of true tomato season, these are usually your best bet.

BEER

Ale vs. Lager

Almost all of the beer in the world can be broken down into two categories: **ales** and **lagers**. If you've sampled the array of brews on offer at your local bodega, you're likely familiar with the difference already: lagers are the crisp chuggables like Budweiser and Miller Light, while ales are the richer, more full-flavored beers like stouts, IPAs, and saisons.

While there are many variables in beer-making—including the kind of grains the beer is made with (Budweiser has rice in it!) and the quantity and type of hops (some taste kind of like weed!)—the functional difference between the two categories lies in the strain of yeast used to make them.

Like wine (page 203), bread (page 1), and pickles (page 162), beer relies on yeast for fermentation: it's how the sugars in the malted grain (grain that's started to sprout) get converted into alcohol. The yeast used in **ales**, *Saccharomyces cerevisiae*, thrives at warm-ish temperatures (around 70°F) and rises to the top of the liquid as it ferments. **Lager** yeast, *Saccharomyces pastorianus*, sinks to the bottom of the liquid as it ferments and works slower and at a cooler temperature (50°F) than ale yeast. Lagers were originally fermented in caves during the cold months and consumed in the spring, when the weather warmed up and the yeast was done with its job. That's why lagers are called lagers—the name comes from the German word *lagern*, which means "to store."

The advent of refrigeration and their thirst-quenching capabilities have made lagers the dominant global style of beer. But they're more expensive to make: you need time, storage, and a cooling system. That's why craft breweries almost exclusively produce ales—they're less of a cash suck than lagers and can be fermented, hopped, and canned in just a few weeks.

IPA vs. Pale Ale vs. Pilsner vs. Saison vs. Wheat Beer

Now that you've got ales and lagers down, here are some of the more common (and confusing!) types of beer you'll come across.

IPAs (India Pale Ales)

Dudes who fancy themselves connoisseurs love an IPA: a type of amber-colored ale that gets its flavor from hops, a cone-shaped flower related to cannabis. Depending on the type of hops used and when in the brewing process they're added, they can lend bitter, citrusy, floral, herbal, and/or piney notes to the final product. When it comes to ABV, these beers can get you pretty drunk: the lower-alcohol varieties are around 4–6 percent, but double IPAs—which have a higher hop concentration—can get as high as 10 percent. Brace yourself.

Pale Ales

Pale ales strike a balance between malt and hops, rendering a more medium-bodied beer. They also have a lower ABV than IPAs—around 4–7 percent—which makes it easier to drink more of them.

Saisons (Farmhouse Ales)

Saisons, which range from pale orange to deep amber in color, hail from Belgium. They were traditionally brewed at the end of the cold season before refrigeration was a thing, which meant they had to be both hardy enough to last the summer and thirst-quenching enough to drink in the heat. The result: a fruity, citrusy, perky brew with some malty and hoppy flavors in the mix.

Pilsners

Pilsners are lagers with additional hops, which give them more flavor than Bud Light or PBR. The original pilsners are Czech and are darker and more bitter than the ones from Germany, which are sometimes referred to as "Pils."

Wheat Beers

Wheat beers include at least 50 percent wheat in the malt mix, giving the brew a fruity, floral, yeasty flavor. The protein in the wheat also makes the beer cloudy and lighter in color than many other ales. These are on the lower end of the ABV scale—around 3–7 percent—and are great summer beers: the citrus-banana notes and relative lightness make them particularly refreshing.

Stout vs. Porter

The most famous stout out there is Guinness, the dark, Irish export sucked down in pubs named McGilligan's and McGinley's and McGraw's around the world. But before Arthur Guinness created his namesake beer, he popularized the porter.

The original **porter** was born in the early 1700s in London, supposedly the result of blending stale beer with fresh, hoppy ales to make something pleasant to drink. The brew was eventually reverse engineered to create a standalone version and made famous by Guinness at the end of the century. These days, modern English porters come in two styles: brown and robust. Brown porters are more malty than hoppy, with hints of caramel and chocolate, while robust porters are stronger, with roasted-coffee flavors and a darker color.

Back to eighteenth-century Britain. In the late 1700s, Arthur Guinness started tinkering with the porter recipe, aiming for something darker, stronger, and "stouter." The result: **stout**, a dark brown–to–black beer with more depth than its older sibling, thanks to roasted barley in the grain mix. Now, stouts can run the spectrum of dry to sweet, but you'll get hints of chocolate, toffee, and coffee in all of them. The carbonation is typically low, so the carbon dioxide gets supplemented with nitrogen, giving the beer finer bubbles and a creamier mouth-feel.

Seems simple, right? Never. Because over the past ten years, people started using the terms "stout" and "porter" interchangeably to refer to any dark, richly flavored style of beer. Now, some robust porters contain a fair amount of roasted barley, and one brewery's porter could be stronger than another brewery's stout. Good news: if you're into one type, you'll probably like the other, so best to just taste around and see what you like best.

Belgian Waffle vs. Liège Waffle

If you've ever been to an American diner or a chain hotel or an all-you-can-eat buffet, you've probably had a **Belgian waffle**. But in Belgium, you'd be hard-pressed to spot a "Belgian waffle" anywhere—you'll find **Brussels waffles** and **Liège waffles**.

Brussels waffles are what we think of as Belgian waffles: fluffy, pale, and golden, with deep grooves to catch toppings. The batter is usually leavened with baking powder, not yeast, which makes them easy to whip up for a last-minute breakfast. These waffles might not have a ton of flavor on their own, but they're excellent vehicles for whipped cream, syrup, strawberries, M&Ms, and whatever other delicacies you desire.

A **Liège waffle** is the Brussels waffle's cousin who spent a year abroad and came back with a hot boyfriend and a killer haircut. She's made with a yeasted brioche dough, has chunks of half-melted pearl sugar studded throughout, and possesses enough structure on her own to be eaten as a hand-held snack. Liège waffles are best served with no toppings, and a good one is just as good cold. (The thought of a cold Brussels/Belgian waffle, on the other hand, fills me with despair.)

In Belgium, Liège waffles are a lot more popular, which makes it strange that we think of Brussels waffles as "Belgian." Then again, it's pretty strange that we top our waffles with Oreos and gummy bears, but that doesn't make them any less delicious.

Betty vs. Buckle vs. Cobbler vs. Crisp vs. Crumble vs. Pandowdy

Cobbler

A mess of fruit topped—or "cobbled"—with biscuit dough, pie dough, or cake batter and then baked. Some old-fashioned variations of cobbler are inverted before serving, so the biscuity stuff ends up on the bottom.

Crumble

A deep-dish fruit dessert topped with a streusel made of butter, flour, oats, and sometimes nuts.

Crisp

A crumble but with no oats in the streusel.

Betty

A casserole made with layers of fruit and buttered bread crumbs and baked.

Buckle

A fruit-studded coffee cake with a streusel topping. According to my research, the streusel can be made either with oats or without oats.

Boy Bait

A buckle but without a streusel topping.

Grunt

A biscuit, pie, or cake-topped fruit dessert that's cooked in a covered Dutch oven or cast-iron skillet on the stove. Grunts are very similar to cobblers, but they are steamed instead of baked.

Slump

What people in New England call a cobbler.

Pandowdy

Similar to a cobbler, but the biscuit or pie dough is rolled out and placed on top of the fruit. During the baking process, the topping is broken up with a knife or spoon and pushed into the fruit, causing the filling to bubble over it.

Schlumpf

The only time I've heard of a schlumpf is through a dear friend, who has a delicious blueberry schlumpf recipe. It's technically a crisp, but let this serve as a reminder that you can essentially make up any name for any of these types of desserts and it'll sound about right.

Bonus Entry: Shortcake

A combination of lightly sweetened biscuits, whipped cream, and fresh fruit, prepared separately and layered together for serving. Its components are similar to that of a cobbler (fruit + biscuit), but the fruit is not cooked and the biscuits are prepared on their own, rather than dolloped on top of the fruit mixture before baking.

Bircher Muesli vs. Muesli vs. Overnight Oats

If you've ever had breakfast in a European or pretending-to-be-European hotel, you've likely heard of Bircher muesli. And if you frequented the wellness blogs of the early 2010s or follow any number of maddeningly sculpturesque fitness influencers on Instagram, you're likely familiar with overnight oats. Two very different contexts, yes, but don't the items seem . . . the same? Like a bunch of soggy, mushy stuff with a vague veneer of health?

That's pretty much the gist of **Bircher muesli**, which was invented by the Swiss nutritionist Dr. Maximilian Bircher-Benner near the end of the nineteenth century. He believed that apples had cured him of jaundice when he was young and was therefore super into fruits and vegetables, an unconventional stance at the time. His muesli was a way of working more fresh fruit into his patients' diets at the Zurich sanatorium where he worked. The original recipe called for 1 tablespoon of raw oats, left to soak in 3 tablespoons of water for twelve hours; 1 tablespoon of sweetened condensed milk; 1 tablespoon of lemon juice; 1–2 apples, freshly grated; and 1 tablespoon of ground hazelnuts or almonds. Now, "Bircher muesli" often refers to any breakfast dish that involves oats soaked in some sort of liquid (water, milk, cream, juice, etc.); additional dairy in the form of milk, cream, or yogurt; grated apple; nuts; dried and/or additional fresh fruit; and optional sweeteners and/or flavorings, such as honey, brown sugar, lemon juice, and vanilla.

Over the years, **"muesli"**—without the "Bircher" prefix—became divorced from its original wetness and came to refer to a dry mixture of raw or toasted grains (usually oats but sometimes millet, barley, rye, etc.), dried fruit, nuts, wheat germ, and bran. It's usually eaten *with* milk, yogurt, and/or fruit juice, but the liquid is not attached to the definition.

So isn't that just . . . **granola**? Not exactly. In most granolas, grains and nuts are toasted with oil and a sweetener like honey, maple syrup, or sugar, making it a sweeter and crunchier product than muesli.

Overnight oats, like Bircher muesli, are all about the sog. They're made of oats soaked in some sort of liquid—usually milk or, more like, some sort of alternative milk—and garnished with the same sort of things you'd find atop Dr. Bircher-Benner's concoction: nuts and/or nut butters, yogurt, dried and fresh fruit, honey, vanilla, etc. Sometimes, chia seeds are added to the base, which I feel like Maximilian would be into if those had been trendy back then. In short: overnight oats are really just a rebranding of Bircher muesli, without the grated apples and the sanatorium vibes. Whatever you call them, they're a pretty delicious breakfast.

Bisque vs. Chowder

A **bisque** is a thick, rich soup, usually made with pureed seafood and milk or cream. The key to a bisque is its smooth consistency: the pure expanse should be unmarred by chunks, though you'll often see garnishes used as a textural contrast.

A **chowder** is the bisque's rougher, edgier cousin: it's chunky by definition, thick with seafood and/or vegetables. Like bisques, chowders often contain milk or cream—Manhattan clam chowder being a notable exception. The name comes from the French word *chaudiere*, the name for the cauldron that fishermen made their seafood stews in.

Blanching vs. Boiling vs. Poaching vs. Simmering

When we talk about **boiling** in cooking, we're talking about big, fat, rolling bubbles, the ones rumbling up to the surface one after another. This is how you want your water when cooking pasta, for example; the constant movement will keep the noodles from sticking to one another.

When it comes to what's going on at the stovetop, **blanching** is the same thing as boiling. However, the term "blanching" implies the stoppage of cooking at the end of the boiling process, usually by shocking the food in ice water or moving it to a baking sheet to cool.

Simmering is a gentler technique than boiling: the bubbles are smaller, and the temperature of the liquid is lower. (Water simmers between 180°F and 205°F, rather than the 212°F of a boil.) The water should be "barely bubbling, like a just-poured glass of your favorite sparkling water, beer, or champagne," writes Samin Nosrat in her book *Salt, Fat, Acid, Heat*. Meats that are simmered fare better than those that are boiled; the lower temperature allows them to cook through evenly without toughening up. Hardier vegetables, such as potatoes and beets, do well in a simmer-bath too. And stocks are simmered so the fats and impurities in the meat float to the top, where they get can get skimmed off rather than churned back in.

Poaching and **coddling** are done at an even lower temperature, with smaller, lazier bubbles. "If simmering water resembles a glass of champagne, then the water for poaching and coddling should look like a glass of champagne you poured last night but (somehow) forgot to drink," writes Nosrat. When foods are poached, they're done so directly in liquid, while coddled foods are cooked in some sort of a container. To make a poached egg, for example, you add a cracked egg directly into the bath, while a coddled egg is cooked in its own shell or in a cute little egg-coddling cup.

Blue vs. Dungeness vs. Jonah vs. King vs. Snow vs. Stone Crabs

There are over 4,500 species of crab on this planet, from the nickel-sized ones skittering out from overturned pebbles at the beach to the monsters of the Bering Sea with a five-foot claw-span. But only a handful of varieties are subjected to the sad fate of being mauled and cracked and picked at by bib-wearing revelers. Here's a breakdown of what could end up on your plate.

Blue crabs are medium-sized specimens found in the Gulf of Mexico and along the Atlantic coast of North America, particularly in the Chesapeake Bay. (Their scientific name, *Callinectes sapidus*, is actually quite lovely: "Callinectes" means "beautiful swimmer," and "sapidus" means "delicious.") They have a gray body, bright-blue claws and legs, and tender, sweet, stark-white meat, which mostly comes from the body rather than its appendages. This is the type of crab you'd douse in Old Bay and attack with mallets on summer vacation in Maryland, and also what's likely in your crab cake at a landlocked steak-house. Also notable: most **soft-shell crabs** in the U.S., available from April to July, are actually blue crabs, captured right as they shed their winter shell and before they grow a new one.

Dungeness crabs, *Cancer magister*, are found along the West Coast, all the way from Mexico up to Canada. They're around one to four pounds, and their fan-shaped shell can grow to up to ten inches in diameter. You'll find its pinkish flesh—which is particularly sweet and delicate—in the body, legs, and claws.

Jonah crabs, *Cancer borealis*, are found off the East Coast, from South Carolina to Nova Scotia. Their bodies measure around seven inches across, but they're prized for their claw meat. Lucky for them, they can actually regrow their appendages, a skill that some fishermen take advantage of: rather than capturing a crab whole and depleting the population, they'll catch one, break off a leg, and throw the rest of it back into the sea.

The **stone crab**, *Menippe mercenaria*, is a softball-sized, reddish-brown specimen that inhabits the warm waters of the Caribbean and the Atlantic coast up to North Carolina. Like Jonah crabs, they have a knack for regenerating their legs—so fishermen will catch them, remove a large "crusher claw," and set them free again, and an even-larger claw will grow back in its place within a year. Since the raw meat tends to stick to the shell, the claws are cooked immediately after they're harvested; you'll usually find them frozen.

Let's move on to the big boys. **Snow crabs**, prized for their long, spindly legs, come from the northwest Pacific and northwest Atlantic, from Alaska to Siberia and Greenland to Newfoundland. They can measure three feet across, legs included, and have white flesh that's tinged with pink. **King crabs** can weigh up to twenty-four pounds, a pretty terrifying thought, and are found in the northern Pacific near Alaska and Japan. Their meat is snowy-white and outlined in red, and their leg span can reach five feet. Get your hands on one of those claws, and you'll really feel like a royal.

Bourbon vs. Rye vs. Scotch vs. Whiskey vs. Whisky

Whiskey (or whisky) is the name for the wide range of liquors made from grains—think corn, barley, rye, or wheat. It's produced by

1. crushing the grains,

2. adding water to make a "mash,"

3. boiling the mixture and letting it cool,

4. adding yeast, which eats the sugars and creates alcohol,

5. draining the resulting liquid (called a "wash") and distilling it in a still, which involves heating the wash, collecting the vapors, then cooling the vapors back into a liquid, and

6. aging that liquid in wooden barrels, usually oak

The difference between **whiskey** and **whisky** is simply where the stuff is made. In the United States and Ireland, it's spelled "whiskey"; in Scotland, Canada, and Japan, it's "whisky." **Scotch**, **bourbon**, and **rye** all fall within the whiskey/whisky category—the differences are in the type of grain, the fermentation process, and where the liquor is made.

Scotch is a whisky (no e!) that's known for its smokiness; you can tell the spirit you're dealing with by getting a whiff. To make it, the grain—usually malted barley (barley that's been steeped in water until it sprouts)—gets heated over a fire made out of the spongy, partially decayed plant matter found in a bog, also known as "peat." The smoke from that fire gives the liquor its distinctive flavor, and different plants within the peat (whether it's mossier or woodier, for example) can actually impart certain characteristics. A whisky can't be called Scotch unless it is entirely produced and bottled in Scotland, and it must be aged for at least three years in oak.

A single-malt Scotch must be made with 100 percent barley and produced at a single distillery in a single season, while blended Scotches incorporate different grains and whiskys from various distilleries. Malts from the Highlands are thought to be the most balanced, Lowland malts are the lightest, and Islay malts are the most robust.

Bourbon is a whiskey made with a mash that's at least 51 percent corn. It involves a sour-mash process, where the grain mixture includes a portion that's already been fermented. Bourbon was first made in Kentucky and, by law, a whiskey can only be called bourbon if it's made in the United States.

In the U.S., **rye whiskey** must be made with a mash of at least 51 percent rye grain; in Canada, however, there's no minimum percentage. Rye is more astringent than bourbon and Scotch, making it particularly well-suited for cocktails.

When consuming any whiskey or whisky, many spirits professionals recommend adding a little water to the glass; the teeny amount of dilution counteracts the alcohol's numbing effect on the senses, helping you smell and taste more of the spirit's flavors.

Broccolini vs. Broccoli Rabe vs. Chinese Broccoli

Chinese broccoli, also known as *gai-lan, kai-lan,* or Chinese kale, is a member of the species *Brassica oleracea,* the same species as regular broccoli, cabbage, and cauliflower. Its cultivar group, the formal category in the International Code of Nomenclature for Cultivated Plants, is called "alboglabra," which sounds completely made up and/or like something out of *Harry Potter* or *Lord of the Rings.* The vegetable has thick stems, itty-bitty florets, and large, flat leaves, and its flavor is somehow stronger and more broccoli-esque than regular broccoli.

Broccolini is a hybrid vegetable, a cross between broccoli and Chinese broccoli that was invented in 1993. It was first grown under the name **"Asparation"** because of its asparagus-flavor undertones, but then some genius was like, "That is a truly horrible name for a vegetable," and decided to market it as "Broccolini" instead. Broccolini/Asparation has a long, leggy stem, small florets, and small, if any, leaves, and it is more tender and sweeter than either of its parents.

Lastly, we have **broccoli rabe**, also known as rapini, which is not a broccoli derivative at all and is instead more closely related to the turnip. It's a bitter green, similar to a mustard green, with thin stalks, little buds, and lots and lots of leaves. It's particularly prevalent in Italian cooking, where it's often blanched (see page 47) and sautéed with olive oil and garlic.

Come March or April, you may start seeing "overwintered broccoli rabe" at the farmers' market, which is broccoli rabe that was planted in the fall and then harvested in the early spring. It's not as large and leafy as normal-wintered rabe, but the leaves and stalks are more tender and less bitter; the vegetable produces extra sugar to keep from freezing. Look for it at your local farmers' market as the weather starts to turn, if it's your *asparation* to cook it.

Broth vs. Stock

Stocks and broths are wondrous examples of basic kitchen alchemy: throw some stuff in a pot of hot water, let it simmer for a while, and out comes a fragrant, wholesome elixir.

Stock is the heavier of the two liquids. It's made by cooking meat bones and water, sometimes with vegetables and herbs, for at least two hours. Sometimes the bones are roasted beforehand, which makes for a deeper-colored stock. The end result: a rich, slightly viscous liquid, thanks to the collagen from the bones and joints, that cools into a kind of meat Jell-O. Stock is never seasoned and is used as an ingredient in other dishes, such as soups, stews, sauces, or as a base for cooking grains.

You get **consomme** by clarifying stock, a process that involves stirring an egg white–water mixture into the pot: the cloudy impurities in the stock attach themselves to the egg whites and rise to the top, where they can then be skimmed off. The resulting liquid is seasoned and often served by itself at the start of the meal.

Broth is made with fewer bones (or no bones!) and more meat than stock, and it often includes vegetables and aromatics. It cooks for a shorter amount of time—under two hours—and is therefore lighter, cooling to a liquid rather than a jelly. Unlike stock, broth is seasoned, which means it can be sipped on its own.

And what about **bone broth**? That's just seasoned stock, which renders it sippable and evidently worth charging an arm and a leg for at your local trendy health-food shop.

Button

Cremini

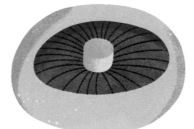

Portobello

Button vs. Cremini vs. Portobello Mushrooms

Let me guess—you almost turned the page. *I obviously know the difference*, you said to yourself. *They are literally just different types of mushrooms.*

I am about to rock your world: THEY ARE NOT. THEY ARE LITERALLY THE SAME TYPE OF MUSHROOM.

They are all *Agaricus bisporus*, in fact, just different ages: **button mushrooms**, which are white, are the toddlers; **cremini mushrooms**, which are brown, are the teenagers; and **portobellos**, which are brown and much larger versions of their younger selves, are the adults. (You know how creminis are sometimes labeled as "baby bellas?" They're literally baby 'bellos!)

Some more fun *Agaricus bisporus* facts:

- They account for 90 percent of the mushroom production in the United States, an almost billion-dollar industry.

- As the mushrooms mature, they lose some of their water content, making portobellos the most flavorful of the bunch (followed by the creminis, then the buttons).

- The average American consumes more than two pounds of mushrooms each year.

- Mushrooms are more closely related in DNA to humans than to plants.

- A single portobello mushroom can contain more potassium than a banana.

Cage-Free vs. Free-Range vs. Hormone-Free vs. Local vs. Pasture-Raised vs. Vegetarian-Fed Eggs

Unless you have a chicken coop in your backyard or the budget for farm-fresh eggs every day, you've probably spent some time in the supermarket's egg aisle. And if you're spending time in the supermarket egg aisle, you're probably familiar with the assault of qualifiers and descriptors—Cage-free! Hormone-free! Free-range! Local!—that awaits you there. Here's what they all mean, and how to navigate them efficiently.

Cage-free, a term regulated by the USDA, means that the eggs come from hens that, quite literally, aren't caged: they can "freely roam a building, room, or enclosed area with unlimited access to food and fresh water during their production cycle, but [do] not have access to the outdoors." Considering the conventional cage is 8.5 by 11 inches, or the size of a piece of paper, that seems like a better lifestyle—but there are caveats. According to Rachel Khong's *All About Eggs*, cage-free facilities have more hen-on-hen violence and lower air quality than facilities that use cages.

Free-range, another USDA term, means that the eggs come from hens that have some sort of access to the outdoors. However, that doesn't mean the hens actually *go* outdoors, or that the outdoor space is more than just a small, fenced-in area with a netted cover.

Pasture-raised is not a term regulated by the USDA; however, if the carton says "pasture-raised" and also includes stamps that say "Certified Humane" and/or "Animal Welfare Approved," it means that each hen was given 108 square feet of outdoor space, as well as barn space indoors. This is pretty much as close to the bucolic farm vibe you'll get when dealing with large-scale egg producers, so if you're looking to support those practices, keep a look out for the labels.

For eggs to be **local**, they must come from a flock located less than four hundred miles from the processing facility or within the same state. And for eggs to be **organic**, the only stipulation is that they must come from hens who are fed an organic diet. Amount of space per hen, access to the outdoors—neither of those are specified or required, though many organic eggs are also at least free-range.

When it comes to eggs labeled **vegetarian-fed**, it's worth noting that chickens are actually omnivorous; they love worms and bugs and larvae and other crawly things. However, in the mass-scale production sense, they're not doing Whole30—they're getting fed animal byproducts, like feather meal or chicken litter. So, depending on the context, vegetarian-fed can actually be the lesser of two evils.

Hormone-free means that the hen wasn't administered hormones, which isn't particularly commendable—considering that hormones and steroids are already banned by the FDA. **No Added Antibiotics** is another funny term, because very few hens are administered antibiotics—and those that do end up being "diverted from human consumption" anyways.

So, given all of this information . . . what should you buy? Cartons stamped with the **Certified Humane** or **Animal Welfare Approved** seal are good bets—both of which are administered by third-party groups. When it comes to brands, Vital Farms, Oliver's Organic, Happy Egg Co., and Pete and Gerry's all have particularly good reputations, as well as Safeway's cage-free eggs and Kirkland organic eggs at Costco.

Calzone vs. Stromboli

There are some pretty iconic mother-child duos out there. Mary and Jesus, for one. Rory and Lorelai Gilmore. The mom and daughter in *Mamma Mia*. Joining the ranks: pizza and her large adult sons, **calzone** and **stromboli**.

And while the two boys certainly take after their mother—they're all made up of dough, cheese, and sauce, and the toppings you'd find on Mom live inside their bellies—their traits present in different ways. Here's how to tell them apart.

Seal

A calzone is folded in half, with its edges crimped (like a dumpling). A stromboli is rolled into a spiral (like a burrito), then sealed off with more dough.

Shape

A calzone is shaped like a half moon. A stromboli looks like an elongated rectangle, with rounded edges.

Cooking Method

Stromboli are baked. Calzones can be baked or fried.

Serving Size

Calzones generally serve one or two people. Stromboli serve a party.

Origin

Calzones were born in Naples, Italy, as a more-portable alternative to pizza. Stromboli come from South Philly and, depending on who you ask, are either named after the 1950 Roberto Rossellini film *Stromboli* starring Ingrid Bergman or after the Isle of Stromboli, home to a volcano named Mount Stromboli that has been erupting almost continuously since 1932 and is one of the most active volcanoes on Earth.

Filling

Both can be filled with pretty much anything: cheese, meat, vegetables, etc. Calzones usually include ricotta, and stromboli usually include mozzarella.

Sauce

You'll rarely find sauce inside a calzone's pocket; it's instead served in a separate vessel for dipping. Stromboli oftentimes have sauce in their filling, but they can be served with a sidecar, too.

Canola vs. Corn vs. Grapeseed vs. Peanut vs. Safflower vs. Vegetable Oils

If you're anything like me, when you get to the flavorless oil section of a supermarket, you simply seek out the cheapest option and move on. There's no pause to consider: *Is a canola a plant?* Or, *What's a safflower?* Or, *Why do I spend time hemming and hawing over the type of olive oil to get, but feel absolutely dead inside when faced with this pale stuff?*

Even my therapist would agree that this lack of emotion is justified. Neutral oils don't taste like anything. They're boring. But that's what makes them so useful: the absence of proteins and free fatty acids and other chemicals found in aromatic, peppery olive oils gives the neutral ones a higher smoke point, allowing them to withstand the high temperatures (up to 450°F) needed to brown, crisp, and fry foods. The darker and more flavorful an oil is—those fancy olive oils, the sesame oils you administer by the drop—the lower its smoke point, which makes them great for drizzling but not-so-great for cooking with.

The broadest category of neutral oil is **vegetable oil**, which refers to the oils pressed from the seeds, nuts, grains, or fruits of plants (with the exception of olive and specialty oils). Most stuff labeled "vegetable oil" in the United States is soybean oil (which has a smoke point of 450°F) or a blend of several different refined oils. If a recipe calls for it, you can use any of the oils we discuss below.

You're also likely familiar with **canola oil**, which has a smoke point of 400°F. It's made from the rapeseed plant, which is similar to the mustard plant. Canola oil ranks second to olive oil in the amount of monounsaturated fat, which really just means that it's better for you than the other vegetable oils.

Corn oil is made from the germ of the corn kernel and has a smoke point of 450°F. It's mostly found in the U.S., where corn is particularly abundant, and gives a bit of a roasty flavor to foods.

Grapeseed oil actually comes from the tiny seeds in some varieties of grapes, and it's a byproduct of winemaking. It has a smoke point of 435°F.

Peanut oil has the highest smoke point of the bunch—471°F—and is made from pressing steam-cooked peanuts. It's not the same thing as unfiltered peanut oil, which tastes quite deeply of peanuts and is not a great thing to accidentally substitute when making, say, Caesar dressing, which has definitely happened to me.

Lastly, **safflower oil**, with a smoke point of 450°F, is made from the seeds of safflowers. And what is a safflower, you ask? It's a plant in the same family as the sunflower and has red, white, yellow, or orange blooms. The dried petals can be used as a dye, and the meal left over from making oil is repurposed as a protein supplement for livestock. Ah, the circle of life!

Captain vs. Host vs. Maitre D'

Let's say it's Friday night, and instead of reading this book, you're out at the hottest restaurant in the city. Who took your reservation? Who's greeting you at the door, taking your jacket, sending you a glass of bubbly (or dismissing you coolly) when your table's not ready?

The **host** is likely the person who said hello to you at the door and checked your coat. If the restaurant took reservations—and if it's as hot as we're pretending it is, it likely didn't—they were probably the person on the other end of the phone. And when your table is finally ready, they may be escorting you to your seat.

The **maitre d'**, short for the French term "maitre d'hotel," has more responsibility than the host. They oversee the seating chart, make sure any VIPs get taken care of, and manage the flow of customers in and out of the restaurant. If you put up a fuss because your table is taking too long—or if you linger at your table well after paying your check—the maitre d' is likely stepping in to handle the situation. Depending on staffing, they sometimes double as the floor manager, directing the front-of-house operations of the entire restaurant.

The **captain's** role is more focused on the people sitting and eating, rather than the flow in and out of the space. They oversee a group of tables and the diners sitting at them, orchestrating servers, food runners, bussers, and other front-of-house folk as needed. They're also in charge of the pacing of your meal: when your food takes too long to arrive, they're who you're complaining to. These days, however, many restaurants go without captains; they're more of a fixture at formal, older-school places. So unless you're dining at Per Se or Le Bernardin, the servers are probably handling a captain's duties—all the more reason to give them a good tip.

Carpaccio vs. Ceviche vs. Crudo vs. Sashimi vs. Tartare vs. Tiradito

"**Crudo**" is the Italian and Spanish word for "raw," and it refers to a dish of uncooked stuff—usually fish, shellfish, or meat—dressed with olive oil, citrus juice, and/or a vinaigrette. "Crudo" doesn't imply a specific size, shape, or technique involved with how the ingredients are sliced, so it can serve as a blanket term for anything that's raw and dressed.

Carpaccio is a type of crudo, but one in which the uncooked stuff is sliced or pounded super thin. It's oftentimes made with fish, but you'll also see meat or even vegetable carpaccios as well (though calling a salad a "crudo" would be a particularly eye-rolly thing to do). Like others in the crudo category, carpaccios are dressed/drizzled, usually with an olive oil–lemon combo, and anointed with a garnish.

Another type of crudo is **tartare**, which is made of raw meat or seafood that's chopped up and bound with a sauce or dressing. Like carpaccios, tartares are defined by the shape in which the raw stuff is sliced—in this case, minced or diced.

Sashimi is a raw preparation that falls outside the crudo category. It's made with carefully sliced raw fish served unadorned; it's more about the quality of the fish and the technique of the chef preparing it rather than vinaigrettes or seasonings. For classic sashimi, the fish is killed in the manner of *ike jime*, in which a spike is inserted into its brain. This method kills the fish instantly, preventing cortisol, adrenaline, and other stress-related chemicals from being released and preserving its flavor and texture for longer.

While it's not technically raw, it's worth noting a crudo-family cousin: **ceviche**. Ceviche is made of raw seafood marinated in citrus juice, which gives it a texture more akin to something that's been cooked. Standard recipes call for around eight times the amount of acid found in dishes like crudo or tartare, and the seafood hangs out in it for longer. The dish can be found all over Latin America, and the ingredients and garnishes vary by locale; a ceviche in Peru, for example, will look and taste different from a ceviche in Colombia or Mexico.

Tiradito is essentially a mash-up of all the stuff we've talked about; it's made of raw fish, sliced thinly (like carpaccio or sashimi) and then marinated in an acidic mixture (like ceviche). It only cures for twenty or so minutes, however, rather than the longer baths that a ceviche typically takes. Tiradito is a part of Nikkei cuisine, a form of Japanese-Peruvian cooking that evolved after a nineteenth-century influx of Japanese immigrants to Peru. Turns out a lot of cultures have ways of making raw food taste delicious—and that great stuff happens when those traditions intertwine.

Caviar vs. Roe

Roe is a term that refers to all fish eggs; **caviar**, the stuff you eat on special mother-of-pearl spoons and costs $100 (or more!) an ounce, can only come from sturgeon. Caviar has been considered a delicacy since ancient times; according to *The Cook's Essential Kitchen Dictionary*, the Roman emperor Severus had it served to him on a bed of roses while being serenaded by flutes and drums. Its status has shifted over time—in the 1800s, for example, sturgeon would get caught up in commercial fishing nets and were considered worthless—but in recent decades, popularity has soared. In 2006, alarmed by dwindling numbers of Russian sturgeon in the Caspian Sea, the U.N. banned the global trade of caviar—which means the stuff you eat now is likely from farmed sturgeon instead of wild.

The **American white sturgeon** was one of the first caviar-producing fish to be farmed. It has bit of a larger egg and, according to Russ & Daughters co-owner Josh Tupper, has a particularly nutty flavor. **Siberian caviar** is milder and sweeter than American. **Sevruga caviar** has the smallest eggs, which are quick to burst on the tongue. **Osetra caviar** is lighter and larger than the others, and the species, *Acipenser gueldenstaedtii*, takes the longest to produce eggs. (Many connoisseurs consider this to be the best caviar.) The rarest and most expensive type, **beluga caviar**, comes from the sturgeon primarily found in the Caspian sea and is therefore illegal in the U.S. (The only exception: a single farm in Florida has a permit to raise beluga sturgeon and sell its caviar domestically.)

Unlike sturgeon-specific caviar, **roe** can come from all types of fish, including salmon, trout, carp, cod, herring, lumpfish, and mackerel. While you'll find it in a wide range of sizes, textures, and flavors, there are two that could easily pass as caviar: paddlefish and hackleback. Paddlefish roe has a stronger salinity than the real stuff, which makes it great for garnishing eggs and latkes and other cooked dishes—you can actually taste it. Hackleback roe has a milder flavor than paddlefish, and you can enjoy it in the same way you'd enjoy caviar: with crème fraîche and blinis, perhaps, or totally on its own. It'll cost you more than paddlefish, but it's still a fraction of caviar's price.

CHEESE

Burrata vs. Mozzarella vs. Stracciatella

Mozzarella is a fresh cheese made with cow's milk—or, in the case of *mozzarella di bufala*, water-buffalo milk. To produce it, the milk is separated into curds and whey, and the curds get strained, sliced, and submerged in a bath of 180–185°F water. They're kneaded until they're stretchy and elastic, then shaped into smooth, round balls.

You get **stracciatella** when you take strands of fresh mozzarella and soak them in fresh cream; the result is a not-quite-solid, not-quite-liquid luxurious mess that makes a single piece of toast and cheese seem like it's worth $13.

And **burrata** happens when you take a ball of mozzarella and fill it with that very stracciatella, so that what looks like a solid mass of mozzarella ends up oozing a mozzarella-and-cream puddle as soon as you cut into it. Use it for your next caprese salad, and you might never turn back.

Parmigiano-Reggiano vs. Parmesan

America is the birthplace of countless groundbreaking inventions: the lightbulb, the telephone, the airplane, candy corn. And while we're excellent at building things, we're also excellent at ruining them. A prime example: parmesan.

"Parmesan" is technically the English translation of **Parmigiano-Reggiano**, a cow's milk cheese made in Italy with Protected Designation of Origin status, or *Denominazione di Origine Protetta* (DOP). It's known as the "king of cheeses" because it's pretty much perfect: salty and savory but also sweet, crumbly and crunchy and yet somehow ethereal, complex in a way that makes you want to squint into the distance until someone asks if you're OK. The Parmigiano-Reggiano label is strictly regulated by the European Union and must adhere to these standards:

1. It can only be produced in the provinces of Parma, Reggio Emilia, Modena, Bologna, and Mantova.

2. The only ingredients are cow's milk, salt, and rennet (an enzyme from cow intestines that helps coagulate the milk during cheesemaking).

3. The milk used in a given batch must be skimmed milk from the evening before and whole milk from that morning.

4. The milk must come from cows from the Parmigiano-Reggiano production area whose dry food is made of at least 50 percent hay, and at least 75 percent of that hay must come from within the defined borders, and at least 50 percent of that production-area hay must be produced on the farm where the cow itself was born and raised.

5. The wheels must be between 70 and 90 pounds and aged for a minimum of one year.

6. The rind must be stamped with the name, the date it was produced, and the DOP seal. Special seals are placed on wheels that have been aged 18, 24, and 36 months.

In addition to all of the above, the Parmigiano-Reggiano consortium inspects and approves every single wheel once it's been aged for twelve months, to make sure it's good enough for the market.

And then we have what is labeled **"parmesan"** here in the United States, which is any cow's milk cheese with a "hard and brittle rind" and "granular texture" that "grates readily" and has a moisture content of 32 percent or less, according to the FDA. The milk doesn't even need to be whole milk—it can be reconstituted dry milk. There are also no regulations pertaining to the size of the wheel, so producers tend to make them on the smaller side (around ten to twenty pounds) so that they take less time to dry out. And the cheese can be aged for any length of time, so producers can just let it hang until it gets down to the maximum moisture level before distributing it.

The stuff in the cans and jars—you know, with the label "100% Grated Parmesan Cheese"—is even worse. It's certainly not 100 percent cheese; the mixture is cut with cellulose, an anti-clumping agent made from wood pulp. A study by Bloomberg

News in 2016 found that common brands contained up to 8.8 percent of it, whereas an "acceptable" level is more between 2 and 4 percent.

To make sure you're getting the good stuff, look for cheese with the "Parmigiano-Reggiano" label—that's the only term that American "cheese"-makers can't co-opt as their own. It may be pricier than its counterparts, but now you know why.

Chef vs. Cook

Suppose you fancy yourself a culinary genius. You slice and dice and sauté and roast your way to sensual bliss each evening, concocting unforgettable feasts out of the sheer force of your creative prowess. Does that make you a cook or a chef? Well, it depends.

A **chef** is technically a professional cook, someone who runs the kitchen of a restaurant or hotel. They have some sort of codified training, whether it's through culinary school or just working his/her way up through a restaurant kitchen, and there's a management component to the role: it means you're in charge of a kitchen, not just making great food. As cookbook author, TV personality, and Domestic Goddess Nigella Lawson told *Eater*, "Chef means a degree of professionalism either because you've got the qualification or because you've worked in a restaurant kitchen. . . . My only qualification is in Medieval and Modern Languages at Oxford."

Nigella, then, would consider herself a **cook**. In a general, non-restaurant setting, a cook is anyone who prepares food; it has more of an amateur association than the word "chef," simply because it implies the person doesn't cook professionally. (The delineation doesn't come from the actual quality of the food being prepared—you can be a badass home cook that makes better food than someone considered a "chef.") In a restaurant setting, a cook is anyone below the sous chef in the chain of command; they're the people who are literally cooking the food each night, rather than creating recipes and/or managing the kitchen.

Most kitchens operate under some version of the *brigade* system, a model that was devised by Auguste Escoffier over one hundred years ago and is still used today. Here's a very top-level look at the *brigade de cuisine* and the types of cooks and chefs you'll find in a restaurant kitchen.

Chefs
Executive Chef

The top of the food chain. This is the chef who supervises the staff, creates the menu, and manages the business. Depending on the restaurant, this could be more of a figurehead role or someone who is more hands-on.

Chef de Cuisine

The chef who is actively in charge of a kitchen. In smaller restaurants, this can be the same as the executive chef; in larger operations, especially ones with many locations, the chef de cuisine reports to the executive chef, who may not be present every day.

Sous Chefs

The managers of the kitchen. They're the people taking inventory, dealing with invoices, making sure the stations are set up on time, and overseeing the food before it gets sent out into the dining room.

Cooks
Line Cooks/Chefs de Partie

The people who run each station, or a specific realm of the kitchen. These are your *sauciers* (sauce chefs), *rôtisseurs* (meat cooks), *poissonniers* (fish cooks), *entremétiers* (vegetable/soup cooks), and *garde mangers* (the cooks in charge of cold-food preparations, like salads). The *pâtissier*, or pastry chef, is classically a part of this group as well.

Junior Cooks/Commis

The people who work at specific stations under a line cook. They are typically still in training and/or just out of culinary school.

Stagiaires

Usually a student and considered the "intern" of the kitchen. They're usually assigned basic prep tasks, like peeling potatoes or slicing onions.

Also in the brigade system can be the *aboyeur*, who communicates between the front and the back of the house; the *communard*, who prepares staff meal; and the *plongeurs*, or dishwashers.

Cherrystone Clams vs. Chowder Clams vs. Littleneck Clams vs. Razor Clams vs. Steamers vs. Topneck Clams

There are over 150 edible species of clams, and humans have been feasting on them for thousands of years. We know this from examining middens: gigantic piles of ancient shells found on coastlines around the globe, the detritus of history's epic clambakes.

It'd take a whole book to survey the world's clam offerings, but here are the most common types you'll come across.

Chowder Clams, Cherrystones, Topnecks, and Littlenecks

Chowder clams, cherrystones, topnecks, and littlenecks are all the same species: *Mercenaria mercenaria*, also known as "hard shells" or "quahogs." Native Americans used quahog shells as currency, which is where their scientific name comes from: "mercenaria" means "hired for wages." On the Atlantic side of the United States, these clams reign supreme.

Chowder clams are the oldest and largest of the bunch, harvested at around eight years of age. They measure three or more inches across and are anywhere from five ounces and up. These guys are too big and tough to eat raw, so they're chopped up and used in chowders or soups.

Cherrystones fall in the middle of the pack: they're five to

Chowder
Clams

Littleneck
Clams

Cherrystone
Clams

Steamer Clams

Pacific
Razor
Clams

Atlantic Razor Clams

six years old, two to three inches in diameter, and in the two-to four-ounce range. The ones at the bottom of that range are sometimes called topnecks.

And littlenecks are the babies of the family, the smallest, youngest, and most expensive. They're around one to two inches across and one to two ounces each. These are the sweetest and most tender, and are as good eaten raw as they are in a *spaghetti alle vongole*.

Steamers

Steamers, also known as belly clams, Ipswich clams, longneck clams, and piss clams, are from the species *Mya arenaria*. They're described as "soft shells" not because their shells are actually soft, but because they're more brittle than *Mercenaria mercenaria*'s. These are the guys with the long "necks"—actually a double siphon used for breathing and eating—that keep their shells from closing all the way. Thanks to a pantyhose-like layer of skin that grows over the "neck," they're never eaten raw, so you'll see them served steamed or fried.

Steamers live in the wet, mucky intertidal zone that gets exposed during low tide, which gives them a flavor unique to whatever area they come from. The level of acidity of the mud they hang out in actually changes the color of their shells: a darker shell makes for a sweeter clam. Steamers can burrow down farther than other clams—up to eleven inches!—and often spend their adult lives chilling in the same spot. Once the older ones are uprooted, they can't make their way back down.

Razor clams

What we think of as razor clams are actually two different species: *Ensis directus* from the Atlantic and *Siliqua patula* from the Pacific. Both of them have shells that look like straight razors, though the clams themselves are quite different. Atlantic boys are long and skinny, while Pacific razors are fatter and meatier. They look like baby versions of the geoduck, a variety of clam from the U.S. Pacific Northwest with thick, protruding, phallic necks that can be the size of a baseball bat.

Chicken Cutlets vs. Chicken Fingers vs. Chicken Nuggets vs. Chicken Tenders

Ah, the wonders of a boneless, skinless chicken breast: that unsullied expanse of flesh, that somewhat-flavorless-but-still-chickeny-enough-to-know-what-we're-eating taste we know so well, that blank canvas so eager to be sliced and chopped and smashed and bathed in various mixtures of condiments. Chances are, you are deeply familiar with this wonder of the world, as well as its many children: the cutlet, the finger, the tender, and the nugget. But how familiar? As we delight in these shining specimens of breaded-and-fried meat, do we know exactly what we're eating?

Let's start with the simplest concept: **chicken cutlets**. Chicken cutlets are boneless, skinless breasts that have been sliced in half horizontally, creating a thinner piece of meat. They are often pounded even thinner before cooking.

To make **chicken fingers**, chicken breasts are cut into strips. (If you see something referred to as "chicken strips," they are probably chicken fingers.) These are not to be confused with **chicken tenders**, which are made from an actual cut of meat: the pectoralis minor, a small muscle that runs directly under the chicken breast. This is also called the "inner filet."

If we're getting technical, a chicken finger could be made from the chicken breast *or* the inner filet—which means that a chicken tender can be a chicken finger, but not all chicken fingers are chicken tenders.

Lastly, we have **chicken nuggets**. Unlike their pure brethren, chicken nuggets are usually made from chopped and/or processed meat that's then re-formed into a chicken-nugget shape. The meat involved does not have to be breast meat—it could be meat from any part of the chicken. Yup, these are your McNuggets; consume at your own risk.

Chives vs. Scallions vs. Green Onions vs. Leeks vs. Ramps vs. Spring Onions

Before we get into the lesser-known children in the allium family, let's talk about onions. In the U.S., onions are differentiated not by actual species, but by the season they're harvested in. **Spring onions** are planted in the fall and harvested the following spring or summer, when they're still young and immature. They have a little baby bulb at the bottom and long, green shoots growing out of the top. If left in the ground until the fall, they grow into **storage onions**, the ones with dry, papery skin that serve as the backbone of countless dishes and can be held in storage through the winter.

Scallions, also known as **green onions**, look like spring onions without a bulb at the bottom: they grow straight up and down. Particularly young spring onions are sometimes labeled as scallions, but their taste is pretty much indistinguishable—in fact, they're all the same species, *Allium cepa*.

Leeks, *Allium ampeloprasum*, are much larger than scallions, with white and light green bottoms and sturdy, flat, dark-green leaves up top. Most people just eat the bottom sections—the tops are edible, but tough and fibrous. Leeks are most abundant at the end of the fall, though they're so great at withstanding the cold that in certain locales, they can be harvested throughout the winter. Their flavor is more subtle and elegant than the common onion, and when cooked properly, they have an almost silky texture.

Young, wild leeks are called **ramps**, *Allium tricoccum* if you're being fancy. They look a bit like scallions, but with wide,

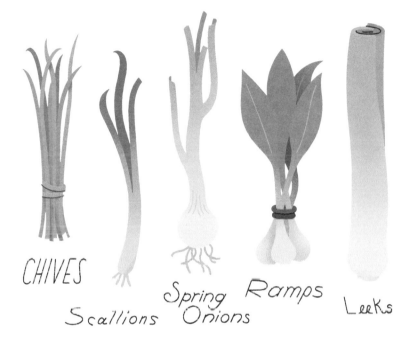

CHIVES

Scallions

Spring
Onions

Ramps

Leeks

flat leaves up top. People go crazy for them in the springtime, where you'll see them pop up on every new-American menu in New York City. They grow like weeds from Quebec down to the Carolinas, but can cost a small fortune at the farmers' market. They taste like a cross between garlic and onions but have a much more pungent smell.

Chives, *Allium schoenoprasum*, are the smallest, skinniest alliums of the bunch. They're considered an herb and have a pleasant, mild oniony flavor. Chives have hollow stems that are easily snipped, and for a time in the spring, they may even have little flowers up top. Just exercise caution if you plant chives in your garden—they grow like weeds and will happily dominate your plot.

Some more fun facts about alliums:

- The Roman emperor Nero used to eat tons of leeks because he believed they would make him a better singer.

- In the sixth century, the Welsh made leeks their national symbol; they thought the leeks they wore pinned to their helmets helped them win battles. Today, it's still traditional in Wales to wear a leek on March 1, a holiday called St. David's Day.

- The sulfur compounds in onions and garlic can actually attach themselves to your clothes and hair—which is why you smell like them long after you're done chopping.

- Chives have been a part of Chinese cooking since 3000 BC and were prized as an antidote to poison.

- The ancient Romans used chives to tell fortunes, but nobody really knows why.

CHOCOLATE

Bittersweet vs. Semisweet Chocolate

To understand the differences between types of chocolate, we must first explore how chocolate is made. Cocoa beans, which grow on trees in pods that look like elongated, accordioned, technicolor lemons, are separated, fermented, dried, roasted, and cracked open. The shells are removed, and the inner meat is milled into a thick paste called chocolate liquor, or "cacao." Pure chocolate, also known as bitter, baking, or unsweetened chocolate, is made of that liquor and sometimes includes flavorings like vanilla or vanillin (synthesized vanilla).

In its natural state, chocolate liquor is about 55 percent cocoa butter; the other 45 percent is made of cocoa solids responsible for chocolate's flavor. The butter and solids can be separated and recombined in different ratios; together, they make up a chocolate bar's cacao percentage, one you've likely seen touted on a label. (If that number isn't indicated, it's likely

53 percent cacao.) The non-cacao stuff in the mix is usually sugar and sometimes a fat called lecithin.

Now that we've gone on this journey together, it's time to break the news: There is no official distinction between **bittersweet** and **semisweet** chocolate. One brand's semisweet and another's bittersweet could have the same exact proportions; the only rule is that they must be made up of at least 35 percent cacao. The best way to tell the difference, then, is to simply taste the stuff you're working with.

Dutch-Processed Cocoa Powder vs. Natural Cocoa Powder

When cocoa butter is extracted from chocolate liquor, you're left with a bunch of crumbly solids; those solids are ground up to make cocoa powder. **Natural cocoa powder** is exactly that, without any extra layers of processing. It has a sharp, astringent, almost citrusy taste, and it's acidic: the pH clocks in between 5 and 6.

Dutch-processed cocoa powder is cocoa powder that's been washed in a potassium solution to neutralize it, stripping it of its acidity and bringing its pH to around 7 or 8. The process makes the powder a deeper brown color, converting the astringent, bitter molecules into flavorless dark pigments. This gives it a more balanced taste and a more "chocolatey" flavor.

In recipes, natural cocoa powder is usually paired with baking soda (page 21); the acidity of the cocoa powder and alkalinity of the baking soda react with each other to create carbon dioxide, allowing whatever you're baking to rise. Dutch-processed cocoa powder is usually used with baking powder; since it's not acidic, it won't react with baking soda. So when making things like cookies, brownies, and cake—any recipe with chemical leavener—you can't swap one in for the other. But with other kinds of desserts, like ice cream or pudding or hot chocolate, it's really a matter of taste: for a richer chocolate flavor, use the Dutch-processed powder; for a lighter, tangier final product, go for the natural stuff.

Hot Cocoa vs. Hot Chocolate

Hot cocoa is made from cocoa powder, sugar, and milk or cream; the ratios are a matter of personal preference. (And if you're more into Swiss Miss, no judgment here.) Since making hot cocoa doesn't involve baking, you can use either natural or Dutch-processed cocoa powder—whatever stirs up those happy-homey-nostalgic feelings more for you. Drinks made with Dutch-processed will taste chocolatier, while natural cocoa will give a brighter, fruitier flavor.

Hot chocolate, also known as "drinking chocolate," is made with real chocolate, either chopped up or shaved and added to hot milk, cream, or water. It's richer and fuller than hot cocoa, and oftentimes less sweet. The drink has been around for 2,500 to 3,000 years; the ancient Mayans would make a beverage out of ground-up cocoa beans and chilies. Try adding some ground chile de arbol or cayenne to your next batch, and you'll be converted.

Chop vs. Dice vs. Mince vs. Slice

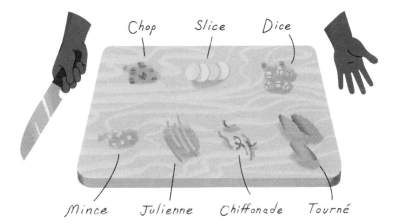

Chop   Slice   Dice

Mince   Julienne   Chiffonade   Tourné

Chop

Chopping involves cutting an ingredient into even hunks. We're not talking perfect squares or half-moons or another form pleasing to the eye—the pieces just need to be around the same size.

Slice

To slice an ingredient is to cut it into thin, broad, even pieces— think tomatoes for a caprese salad, onions before you caramelize them, or a just-rested steak before serving.

Dice

With a dice, foods are cut into neat little cubes so that they cook evenly (and look good). Obviously, this is tough for curvy and bumpy fruits and vegetables—the key is to break those down into what the *New York Times* describes as "cubic shapes" and then cut those pieces along horizontal and vertical lines until you get the size you want. In a large dice, the cubes are around ¾ inch, and in a brunoise (the smallest dice), they're around ⅛ inch.

Mince

In a mince, the pieces are even smaller than a brunoise—but because they're so tiny, they're past the point of being uniform. It's just chopping on a very micro level. To get there, you'll want to get your ingredient down to a small dice, and then go at it a few more times with your knife.

Now that we've covered the basics, let's explore some bonus cuts:

Julienne

Julienning an ingredient just means slicing it super thinly: the pieces should be ⅛- to ¹⁄₁₆-inch thick, around the width of a matchstick.

Chiffonade

A chiffonade is similar to a julienne, but specific to herbs and leafy greens. A wider chiffonade is used for salads, while a skinnier one is used for garnishes.

Tourné

A *tourné* is as fancy as it sounds: a vegetable is cut into a seven-sided football shape using a special knife. More sides means more browning, so this is great for something like potatoes, when you're trying to achieve maximum crispiness. Unless you're cooking old-school French stuff, you won't come across a recipe that calls for the technique, but it's a fun skill to practice nonetheless.

Chutney vs. Compote vs. Jam vs. Jelly vs. Marmalade vs. Preserves

Jam, jelly, preserves, marmalade, compote, and chutney all involve some combination of fruit, sugar, and heat, and they rely on pectin—a natural fiber found in most plants that helps cooked fruit firm up—for texture. The underlying difference between them? How much of the physical fruit is used in the final product.

On one end of the spectrum, we have **jelly**: the firmest and smoothest product of the bunch. Jelly is made from fruit juice, which is usually extracted from cooked, crushed fruit. (That extraction process, which involves straining the fruit mixture through a fine mesh fabric, is also what makes jelly clear.) The resulting juice is then heated with sugar, acid, and oftentimes additional powdered pectin to get a gel-like texture. That cranberry stuff you eat on Thanksgiving, the stuff that slides out of the can in one perfect, ridged cylinder? Definitely jelly.

Next up we have **jam**, which is made from chopped or pureed fruit (rather than fruit juice) cooked down with sugar. Its texture is usually looser and more spoonable than jelly, with seeds or skin sometimes making an appearance. **Chutney** is a type of jam made without any additional pectin and flavored with vinegar and various spices, and it's often found in Indian cuisines.

Preserves contain the most physical fruit of the bunch—either chopped into larger pieces or preserved whole. Sometimes, the preserves are held together in a loose syrup; other times, the liquid is thicker. **Marmalade** is simply the name for preserves made with citrus, since it includes the citrus rinds as well as the inner fruit and pulp. (Citrus rinds contain a ton of pectin, which is why marmalade oftentimes has a firmer texture more akin to jelly.)

Compote, a close cousin to preserves, is made with fresh or dried fruit, cooked low and slow in a sugar syrup so that the pieces stay somewhat intact. However, unlike preserves—which are usually jarred for future use—compote is used straight away.

Here's your cheat sheet:

Jelly: fruit juice + sugar

Jam: chopped or pureed fruit + sugar

Chutney: chopped or pureed fruit + sugar + vinegar + spices

Marmalade: whole citrus (either chopped or left intact) + sugar

Preserves: whole fruit or fruit chunks + sugar

Compote: whole fruit or fruit chunks + sugar (but usually eaten immediately, not preserved)

Cilantro vs. Coriander

Coriander and cilantro refer to the same plant: *Coriandrum sativum.* And while "coriander" technically refers to the plant in its entirety, it's more often used to describe its seeds; the leaves are known as "cilantro."

Coriander seeds have been used for thousands of years; they were found in Bronze Age settlements and in the tomb of King Tut. The name comes from the ancient Greek word for "bedbug"—supposedly the crushed bugs and unripe seeds have a similar smell. In terms of flavor, coriander is floral and fruity and is used to flavor sausages, pickles, stews, baked goods, and more.

Cilantro, or "fresh coriander" if you're in the U.K., are the plant's green, serrated leaves. Originally from the Middle East, according to Harold McGee's *On Food and Cooking,* the plant was taken to China, India, and Southeast Asia and later to Latin America, and the leaves are popular in all of those regions. In Central and South America, cilantro ended up replacing **culantro,** an indigenous relative with a similar flavor but larger, tougher leaves.

Cilantro is a polarizing herb: some people love it, while others say it tastes soapy. And though it's easy to dismiss the soapsters as picky, they're not wrong. According to McGee, the main components of cilantro's aroma are fragments of fat molecules called aldehydes—and similar aldehydes are found in soaps, lotions, and yes, bugs. Some people taste those aldehydes and think they're disgusting, while others don't mind them. Personally, I'm in the cilantro-lover camp—though if I ever smelled crushed bedbugs, I'd probably cross over to the dark side.

Clementines vs. Mandarins vs. Satsumas vs. Tangerines

Mandarins, *Citrus reticulata,* are a whole species of orange fruit, with types that range from the size of a ping-pong ball to a dodgeball. The Citrus Variety Collection of the University of California includes 167 different varieties, which all share a number of characteristics:

1. they're orange,

2. they all have a flattish top and bottom, meaning they won't roll off a table if you leave them unattended, and

3. they have skins that slip off easily, which makes them a dream to peel.

Mandarins are native to southeastern Asia and the Philippines and arrived in the U.S. in the 1840s, when the Italians planted them in their consulate garden in New Orleans. They're named for the color of the robes worn by Chinese mandarins, the term for public officials in the imperial era.

Tangerines, clementines, and **satsumas** are all types of mandarins. **Tangerines** are the most tart of the three, with thick, bumpy, orange skin. They originally came from the port of Tangiers in Morocco—hence the name—and are now most common in North America.

Clementines have a smooth, glossy, thin peel and are sweeter than tangerines. They're usually seedless and come by way of North Africa. Clementines grown in warmer weather often have a higher sugar content, while ones from chillier locales can be more tart. The mandarins you see in the grocery store called Cuties and Sweeties are all clementines.

Satsumas are smaller than clementines, with sweet, pretty-much-seedless flesh and lighter-orange skins. They originated in Japan hundreds of years ago from seedlings brought over from China and now account for 80 percent of Japanese citrus production. The trees are hardy enough to withstand colder weather, and they grow well in the relatively chillier areas of northern Florida and the California Sierra foothills. The canned mandarins in the U.S. are usually satsumas; the fresh ones don't travel particularly well. If you can get your hands on them, you'll notice that they're easier to peel than clementines—and even "cuter" and "sweeter" than them, too.

Club Soda vs. Seltzer vs. Sparkling Mineral Water

Seltzer is simple: it's just plain water, jacked up with carbon dioxide. This is the bubbly stuff that's most likely to come flavored, since it's such a neutral canvas; it's the base for your LaCroix, your Polar, or whatever hint-of-fruity sparkling beverage you're partial to.

Club soda is also carbonated with carbon dioxide, but unlike seltzer, it has potassium bicarbonate and potassium sulfate added to the mix. These minerals give it a slightly saltier taste than seltzer, which makes club soda a favorite of bartenders to use in mixed drinks.

Sparkling mineral water is made with natural spring or well water, which means it has naturally occurring minerals (like salts and sulfur compounds) in it. These minerals sometimes give the water a natural carbonation; other times, carbon dioxide is added for extra oomph. Depending on where the water's from, it might taste heavier than seltzer or club soda—or you may just detect some sort of presence of taste, unlike its more tasteless brethren.

Cappuccino vs. Cortado vs. Flat White vs. Latte vs. Macchiato

Every weekday, around 2 or 3 p.m., one often momentarily breaks free from the desk-chains of capitalism to engage in more capitalism by purchasing an overpriced caffeinated beverage to help one practice capitalism faster. And while you know you want coffee, do you know exactly what you're drinking?

Cappuccinos, lattes, macchiatos, flat whites, and cortados are all defined by their ratios of espresso to milk. The milk can be steamed, which makes it lightly frothy, or foamed, a firmer, airier form that holds its shape.

A **macchiato** has the smallest amount of milk: it's made with a shot or two of espresso with around a half ounce of foam on top. The term means "marked" or "stained" in Italian, and that's the exact use of the dairy here—just a little dab to finish it off.

A **cappuccino** can vary in size, but its ratios are usually the same: one-third espresso, one-third steamed milk, and one-

Flat White

Cortado

Cappuccino

 Espresso

Steamed
milk

Foamed
milk

Latte

Macchiato

third foam. A standard version is six ounces, with two ounces of each—but try telling that to the dude ahead of you at Starbucks, who just ordered a Venti to go.

A **cortado** is made of two ounces of espresso with between one and two ounces of steamed milk, sometimes a tad more. It's served in an actual glass, which means (1) the temperature needs to be a bit cooler than something served in a mug, since you have to grasp the vessel with your hand in order to drink it, and (2) it must be consumed quickly, since you can't take it on the road. A cortado is also sometimes called a **Gibraltar**, named after the type of glass it's served in.

A **flat white**, popularized by our mates in Australia and New Zealand, contains two ounces of espresso with between one and four ounces of steamed milk, depending on who you ask. The real differentiator is the way the milk is steamed: its texture is softer and velvety, allowing it to integrate fully into the drink instead of just sitting on top. Coffee nerds call this "microfoam."

A **latte** is the most milk-heavy of the drinks, comprising two ounces of espresso and between six and twenty (!) ounces of steamed milk. It's often capped by a thin layer of foam on top, no more than a quarter inch in depth—or decorated with a heart or a tree or a self-portrait or an approximation of Van Gogh's *Starry Night*, to be admired before sucking it down.

Cold Brew vs. Iced Coffee

Iced coffee is exactly what it says it is: coffee that's brewed hot, then served over ice. To make it, water is heated to around 200°F and then poured over coffee grounds, where it quickly works its way through the granules and pulls out good-tasting things and caffeine. Ice it down, and you've got iced coffee.

To make **cold brew,** coarse-ground coffee is steeped in cool water for around twelve to twenty-four hours. The grounds are then filtered out, and the resulting coffee concentrate can be mixed with milk, water, and/or ice. Because the process doesn't involve any heat, many of the acids and oils that make coffee taste bitter don't get released—resulting in a sweeter, "smoother" beverage.

The caffeine content in cold brew is generally higher—an average 8-ounce iced coffee has 95 milligrams of caffeine, while a 10.5-ounce Stumptown cold brew stubby, for example, contains around 279 milligrams—and it uses up twice the amount of coffee grounds. The extra beans it takes to produce, plus the longer sitting time, is why cold brew is normally more expensive than regular joe.

And what about **nitro cold brew**, the item on fancy coffeeshop menus with teeth-rattling prices next to it? That's cold brew that's been run through a keg, a process that infuses the coffee with tiny nitrogen bubbles. The resulting drink is rich and frothy, with a foamy cap similar to that of Guinness. Perfect to hold you over until happy hour.

Condensed Milk vs. Evaporated Milk

Evaporated milk and condensed milk start off, unsurprisingly, as fresh milk. To make both products, milk first goes through a vacuum process that evaporates around 60 percent of its water volume, concentrating its proteins, fats, and sugars.

For **evaporated milk**, the super-milk is then poured into cans and heated to prevent spoilage. That sterilization process caramelizes some of the milk sugars, giving the final product a lightly nutty flavor and a beige, ivory hue.

But why would you use evaporated milk over regular milk? "The advantage of using canned dairy in certain recipes is the reduction of moisture," says cookbook author Erin McDowell. "When you add evaporated milk, it produces a creamier, denser product." That translates particularly well to ice cream–making: less water means less ice and a smoother, richer product.

Condensed milk is just evaporated milk with a ton of sugar added to it, up to 2 $\frac{1}{3}$ cups per can. The result is thick, syrupy, and super sweet. Unlike evaporated milk, condensed milk isn't heat-sterilized; the amount of added sugar is enough to prevent bacterial growth. It's mostly used for sweets: boiled down even further for dulce de leche (page 195), used as a jumping-off point for candies and fudge, or mixed with an acid (like lemon or lime juice) for pies and cheesecakes.

Corned Beef vs. Pastrami

While you may have some vague understanding that pastrami and corned beef are two different things, and that one might be better than the other (no comment), you may be stuck on the how or why. Here are the major points of differentiation between the two.

Country of Origin

Pastrami has two possible ancestries: it's either Romanian (where its predecessor, *pastrama*, was made with pork or mutton) or Turkish (where it'd be a descendent of *pastirma*, made with beef). Corned beef hails from Ireland, which is why it's eaten on St. Patrick's Day.

Cut of Meat

Today's corned beef and pastrami are both made from beef, albeit different parts of the animal. Corned beef is made from brisket, which comes from the lower chest of the cow; pastrami is either made from a cut called the deckle, a lean, wide, firm shoulder cut, or the navel, a smaller and juicier section right below the ribs. These days, you may also see pastrami made from brisket.

Brine

Both pastrami and corned beef are brined before they're cooked; they're either rubbed with or submerged in a solution of salt and spices to infuse the meat with more moisture and flavor. The brine for both cuts includes salt, sugar, black pepper, cloves, coriander, bay leaves, juniper berries, and dill, as well as the preservatives sodium nitrate or sodium nitrite.

Spice Mix

Here's when things really start to differ. After the brining process, pastrami gets covered in a mixture of black pepper, coriander, mustard seeds, fennel seeds, and sometimes fresh garlic; that spice coating is what gives it its blackened appearance. Corned beef is left naked.

Cooking Method

Pastrami is smoked over hardwood, oftentimes with a pan of water nearby, which helps keep the meat moist. It's then cooled and steamed before serving. Corned beef is boiled, sometimes with cabbage and other accoutrements in the mix.

Bonus Round

If you've ever been to Montreal, you may be wondering: What does "smoked meat" have to do with all this? Smoked meat is a Canadian specialty that pulls from the same themes as corned beef and pastrami, but has a narrative of its own. It's made with brisket and is brined in a mixture of black pepper, coriander, garlic, and mustard seeds—but with much less sugar than its pastrami and corned beef cousins. It's then smoked, like pastrami, and is best layered onto rye bread with mustard for serving—just like the rest of the family.

Cornmeal vs. Grits vs. Polenta

Sometimes, it's fun to eat things that challenge us: the almost-too-sour pickles that make our mouths pucker, the mapo tofu that makes our tongue and lips and cheeks tingle, the bowl of chili that's so spicy that it causes us physical pain. Other times, it's nice to eat adult baby food. Enter the world of dried-and-ground corn, the stuff that, when simmered with water or milk or stock, becomes a gruel-like porridge that has been soothing humans for millennia.

Both **grits** and **polenta** fall under the heading of **cornmeal**, which is essentially a flour, or "meal," made from dried corn. Cornmeal can be yellow or white, fine, medium, or coarsely ground, each with its own distinct purposes; fine cornmeal, for example, is best used for baking, as its texture won't interfere with the rest of the dish. Conventional cornmeal—most of the stuff you'll find on the grocery-store shelf—is "degerminated," which means the hull and the germ have been removed from the kernels; this creates a shelf-stable product with a somewhat uniform texture. Stone-ground cornmeal, on the other hand, is whole grain; it still has the hull and the oil-rich germ attached, making it more perishable than the standard stuff.

Grits, popular in the American South, are made from coarse-ground or coarser-than-coarse-ground cornmeal, and the term can refer to both the ingredient and the finished dish. Like most of the cornmeal you'll find in the U.S., grits are typically made from dent corn: a variety with a low sugar content, a soft, starchy center, and a particularly pronounced "corn" flavor. Grits can be white or yellow, both of which are traditional;

historically, white grits were popular in the urban ports of the South, while yellow were more popular in rural, inland areas.

The word "**polenta**," like "**grits**," can refer to both an ingredient and a finished dish—though polenta, in Italy, can be made with any type of ground grain or starch, not just corn. The corn the Italians do use, however, is historically different from the corn in most American cornmeal products; instead of dent corn, true polenta is made from a varietal called flint corn, or *otto file*. This type of heirloom corn holds its texture a bit better than dent corn, giving it a slightly different mouthfeel than grits. Purists and nerds: this one's for you.

Although we delight in these nitpicky, hair-splitting differences, let's be honest: you can use coarse-ground cornmeal for grits or polenta, and they will taste just fine. Just stay away from anything labeled "instant" or "quick-cooking"; that stuff is dried, parcooked, and then dried out again, and it tastes like sawdust. Stick with the real deal, and you'll be as golden as that porridge in front of you.

Crème Brûlée vs. Flan vs. Panna Cotta

Before we get into specifics here, we need to talk about custards. According to cookbook author Erin McDowell, there are three types of custards that you learn about in pastry school: stovetop custards, baked custards, and cold-set custards.

Stovetop custards, also known as stirred or boiled custards, are custards that are simmered on the stove until thickened, then chilled to serve. These are your pastry creams, puddings, and *pots de crème*.

Flan and **crème brûlée** fall into the category of baked custards, which are cooked in the oven, often in a water bath, until just gelled. (The water bath keeps the custards from cracking and/or overcooking.) Notably, crème brûlée has a burnt (brûléed) crust of sugar on top, a sweet, golden cap that shatters with the thwack of a spoon. Cheesecake is also a baked custard; it may be cakier than flan or crème brûlée, but it is prepared in a similar manner.

Panna cotta is the third type, a cold-set custard. To make it, ingredients are just briefly heated on a stove until the sugar is dissolved, then set with gelatin and chilled. There's no baking or simmering involved. And unlike flan and crème brûlée, which rely heavily on eggs, panna cotta is eggless and thickened by the protein in the gelatin. That gives the final product a different texture: it's thicker and firmer, holding the indentation of a spoon or fork in a way that the others will not.

The desserts also hail from different countries. Flan is a Spanish specialty that predates the others; it was featured in medieval cooking as far back as the sixth century. Panna cotta was created in nineteenth-century Italy and translates as "cooked cream." And while crème brûlée is well-known in France, it's actually an old English recipe; according to *The Cook's Essential Kitchen Dictionary,* the name was likely made *français* in the eighteenth century by French food–lover Thomas Jefferson.

Crème Fraîche vs. Sour Cream

Sour cream, which has a fat content of around 20 percent, is made by mixing cream with a lactic-acid culture; the bacteria is what makes the dairy thick and sour. Stabilizers like gelatin and rennin are also sometimes included in the mix. It's best to use sour cream cold or at room temperature—it will curdle if you simmer or boil it—or to stir it into a hot dish once it's off the heat. In a pinch, it can be replaced with whole-milk yogurt, which has about 10 percent fat.

Crème fraîche—clocking in at 30 percent fat—is traditionally made with just unpasteurized cream, which naturally contains the bacteria needed to thicken it. However, in the United States, cream must be pasteurized—so crème fraîche is made by mixing cream with fermenting agents that contain the necessary bacteria. You can actually make your own crème fraîche at home: mix together heavy cream and buttermilk, then let it hang out at room temperature until it reaches its desired thickness (around eight to twenty-four hours). As it sits, the bacteria in the milk converts the sugars (lactose) into lactic acid, which lowers the pH of the mixture and prevents the formation of any unwelcome microbes.

Crème fraîche is thicker, richer (see: fat content), and less tangy than sour cream, and since it won't curdle if you boil it, it's great to use in soups and sauces. Or just spoon it into your mouth, unadorned.

Crispy vs. Crunchy

We've all been there: face-up, couch-ridden, jumbo bag of potato chips or Tostitos or salty/carby snack of choice in hand, staring glassy-eyed at the ceiling or at the television or at the computer, contemplating life or heartbreak or truly nothing at all.

But have you ever paused, mid-mastication, to muse: *Is what I'm eating a crispy food or a crunchy food? Is the mechanical force of my jaw and its subsequent auditory output more in line with that of a crisp, or a crunch?*

According to the scholarly article "Critical Evaluation of Crispy and Crunchy Textures: A Review," published in the *International Journal of Food Properties*, a **crispy** food is defined as:

> a dry, rigid food *which, when bitten with the incisors [Ed. Note: the four pointy teeth at the front of your mouth]*, fractures quickly, easily, and totally *while emitting a relatively* loud, high-pitched sound.

On the other hand, a **crunchy** food is defined as:

> a dense-textured food *which, when chewed with the* molars, *undergoes a* series of fractures *while emitting relatively* loud, low-pitched sounds.

So, in non-science speak: crispy foods are bitten with the four pointy teeth at the front of your mouth, while crunchy foods are chewed with the teeth in the back. Crispy foods break easily, while crunchy foods often require more working of the jaw. And the chewing-sound of crispy foods is higher-pitched than the chewing-sound of crunchy foods, the flute to crunchy's bassoon.

Let's apply these definitions to real life. Lay's potato chips? Crispy. Ice? Crunchy. Saltines? Crispy. Those hard, sourdough pretzels? Crunchy. Celery? Both—it snaps cleanly, and also undergoes a series of fractures when chewed.

Enjoy the symphony of snacking!

Dijon vs. English vs. Hot vs. Spicy Brown vs. Whole-Grain vs. Yellow Mustards

When you squirt mustard onto a pastrami sandwich (page 108) or squiggle it onto a hot dog, you're actually using a condiment that dates back to ancient Rome. Cooks at the time would combine ground mustard seeds with a kind of grape juice called "must" to make *mustum ardens*, which English speakers then butchered into the less-regal-sounding "mustard."

The concept behind the condiment remains simple: just mix together mustard seeds and some kind of liquid. The variation in heat, flavor, and appearance comes from:

1. **The type of seeds used:** Yellow seeds are the mildest, while brown and black seeds are more pungent.

2. **How finely those seeds are ground:** When mustard seeds are broken and mixed with liquid, certain enzymes convert into nose-clearing mustard oil. Mustards with whole seeds will therefore be less pungent.

3. **The liquid the seeds are mixed with:** The more acidic the liquid, the longer the heat will last—so mustards made with vinegar have a sustained, lower-key burn, while ones with water will be intense when freshly prepared but lose their pungency quickly.

4. **The temperature of the liquid:** Hot water will deactivate some of the heat-producing enzymes, while cold water will keep them intact.

Here's a breakdown of the most common mustard types you'll see at the grocery store, and how they all differ.

Yellow Mustard

Yellow mustard—the kind you put on your ballpark hot dogs—is made with (you guessed it!) yellow seeds, finely ground and mixed with vinegar and water. Turmeric is often added too, which helps give the mustard its trademark hue. Yellow mustard is on the mild side of the spectrum, though it should still have a distinct pungency.

Spicy Brown Mustard

Spicy brown mustard is made with brown seeds and less vinegar than yellow mustard. The hotter seeds and lower acidity lend it a sharper kick than yellow mustard, helping it cut through the fatty, flavorful deli meats it often accompanies. The bran is also left on the seeds, which don't get fully broken down and give the final product a coarser texture.

Dijon Mustard

Dijon mustard is made with finely ground brown and/or black seeds. Unsurprisingly, it was first concocted in Dijon, France, though the products sold in the U.S. do not have to be produced in the region. The classic recipe combines the mustard seeds with *verjus*, a juice made from unripe grapes, though these days it's often made with white wine. Since verjus and white wine are less acidic than vinegar, Dijon is sharp and spicy, and it works well in salad dressings, mayonnaise (page 3), and other sauce-like dishes where a little can go a long way.

Whole-Grain Mustard

To make whole-grain mustard, brown mustard seeds are ground with wine until a paste forms, giving it a thick, chunky consistency. Because not all the seeds are broken down, it's not as spicy as its cousins, and it's great in situations where you want a bit of texture: mix it into a vinaigrette, smear it on some salmon, or slather it on a sandwich.

Hot Mustard

You'll often find hot mustard—which is made with finely ground brown or black seeds—sold in powdered form, with directions to mix it with cold water at home. That combo gives the mustard a super intense heat, with the spice level peaking at around fifteen minutes and mellowing out the longer it sits. You'll often find hot mustard served with dumplings (page 121) or egg rolls (page 122), and if you've dipped one of those in too much of it, you know the sinus-clearing heat it can pack.

English Mustard

English mustard is a variety of hot mustard, but made with a mixture of yellow and brown seeds. You can buy it bottled, but it's sharpest when you make it yourself—which is why you'll usually find it in powdered form. Like Chinese hot mustard, it delivers a sharp kick, but since it's made with yellow seeds, it's not quite as intense.

Dinner vs. Supper

These days, both "dinner" and "supper" refer to the meal taken at the end of the day. But it wasn't always like this: the use of "dinner" to describe the evening feeding is a relatively new phenomenon.

"Dinner" comes from the Anglo-French word *"disner,"* or "to dine," according to *Merriam-Webster*. Throughout history, it has signified the main meal of the day—which, in the 1700s and 1800s, came around lunchtime. **"Supper"** was the name for the light meal in the evening, often a soup that had been simmering on the stove all day. (The word "supper" can be traced back to the Anglo-French *"supe,"* the noun for "soup.")

But with the rise of industrialization, according to historian Helen Zoe Veit on NPR, people couldn't make it home for a big midday feast anymore. The main meal had to shift to the evening. "Supper" was booted and "dinner" took its place. "Lunch"—a word that can be traced back to the Middle English *"nonshench,"* formed from *"non"* (noon) and *"schench"* (drink)— became the new word for the midday meal, a lighter repast that could be eaten at work.

So when you snarf down your Sweetgreen salad in front of your computer midday instead of heading home for a civilized gathering, you know the history that got you there.

Dumpling vs. Gyoza vs. Potsticker vs. Wonton

Dumplings are dough-wrapped parcels filled with meat, vegetables, fish, seafood—really any kind of savory filling. Nepalese momos, Russian pelmeni, Polish pierogi, Afghan mantu: they're all dumplings, through and through.

Potstickers, wontons, and gyoza are all dumplings, too. **Potstickers** are part of the Chinese *jiaozi* family, a type of dumpling made with wheat dough that originated in the north. They're made using the "steam fry" method, which involves searing the bottoms until bronzed, adding a bit of water to the pan, covering the pan to let the dumplings steam, and then uncovering until the water evaporates and the bottoms are browned and crisp. In China, dumplings cooked in this manner are called *guotie*; when they're boiled, they're called *shuijiao*; and when they're steamed, they're called *zhengjiao*.

Wontons are another type of Chinese dumpling; they have thinner skins and are usually served in broth. If you're buying premade wrappers, wonton skins will be square and dumpling wrappers will be round.

Gyoza are Japan's answer to potstickers. They're longer and more svelte than Chinese guotie, with a thinner wrapper and a more finely textured filling. Gyoza are also more dainty than jiaozi, typically two-bite affairs instead of three or four.

Egg Roll vs. Spring Roll vs. Summer Roll

Spring rolls hail from China, and they have super-thin wrappers made from flour and water that turn shatteringly crisp when fried. Their fillings usually include a combination of pork, shrimp, bean sprouts, and cabbage, and they come with a side of vinegar (for the Shanghainese versions) or plum sauce, sweet-and-sour sauce, and/or a Worcestershire-based dipping sauce (for the Cantonese versions). According to the *Chicago Tribune*, spring rolls were originally made for Chinese New Year banquets and stacked to look like bars of gold; they got the name "spring roll" because, in the lunar calendar, the New Year marks the start of spring.

The Chinese spring roll is one of many similar dishes across Asia. These might not be "spring rolls" in name, but they share many characteristics: *cha gio* in Vietnam, which have rice-paper wrappers; *popia thot* in Thailand, which are usually filled with glass noodles, bean sprouts, and wood-ear mushrooms; *lumpia Shanghai* in the Philippines, which are skinnier and longer than other types of spring rolls; *lumpia Semarang* in Indonesia, which are filled with shrimp or chicken.

The **egg roll** is a spring-roll variant created in the U.S.; Andrew Coe's book *Chop Suey: A Cultural History of Chinese Food in the United States* pinpoints its invention in New York by a cook named Lum Fong in the 1930s. The key difference is the addition of egg to the wrapper batter, which gives it a bumpy, blistered look when fried, rather than the smooth-shelled spring roll. Egg rolls are usually filled with cabbage and roast pork and sometimes include minced bamboo shoots and/or water chestnuts. You'll find them served with a side of duck sauce, sweet-and-sour sauce, soy sauce (page 188), and/or hot mustard (page 117).

Summer rolls are Vietnamese in origin, and unlike their spring- and egg-roll cousins, they're not fried and are filled with raw ingredients—which is why they are also sold as "salad rolls." (You may also see them on a menu as "fresh spring rolls.") They consist of a rice-paper wrapper filled with vermicelli noodles, carrots, lettuce, cucumbers, herbs like mint, cilantro, or Thai basil, and shrimp or pork, and they're usually accompanied by a peanut dipping sauce, hoisin sauce, or sriracha.

Entrée vs. Main Course

If "entrée" means "entry" in French, then why do we use the word to refer to a meal's main course? Did something get lost in translation? Is it an attempt at sophistication gone embarrassingly wrong?

In eighteenth-century Britain, a typical upper-class formal dinner was made up of soup, fish, roasted meat, and dessert courses, with bonus additions—sides, salads, cheese—often included. Between the fish and roast came a small dish that, according to a manual from the time, should be "easy to eat and pleasing to the appetite but not satisfying." That mini course—the prelude to the meal's main event—was called an **entrée**.

As dining practices changed, meals got simpler. Four- to five-course dinners were no longer the usual. But the name for the dish that came after the appetizer stuck—even if that "entrée" was actually the roast itself. According to the editors of *Merriam-Webster*, the now-established practice of using "entrée" to mean the **main course** was led by hotels and restaurants. It didn't hurt that the word was obviously French, and "anything French was considered to have prestige."

So yes, calling the main course an "entrée" actually may have been a failed attempt at sounding fancy. But the defancification of the actual meals—paring down those multi-course bonanzas into something more manageable—ended up being a good thing, making dining more accessible and reflecting the broader changes in society as a whole.

Fillet vs. Filet

These words are so similar in both spelling and meaning that someone should just decide on one of them and let us move on with our lives. But they both exist, and they both are used, and so we must persevere.

Fillet is both a noun and a verb; as a verb, it describes the art of cutting meat or fish off the bone, and as a noun, it refers to the resulting piece of boneless meat or fish. **Filet** means pretty much the same thing as "fillet" in its noun form, but can also specifically refer to the filet mignon, a type of steak cut from the beef tenderloin.

I'd love to say that "fillet" is more often used for fish and "filet" for meat—but McDonald's has its Filet-O-Fish®, not a Fillet-O-Fish®, which kills my argument. Long story short: you can use the two words interchangeably, and you'll be correct either time.

Frosting vs. Glaze vs. Icing

This is a tough one. According to multiple dictionaries—including the food-specific *Cook's Essential Kitchen Dictionary* and the *New Food Lover's Companion*—**frosting** and **icing** are the same thing: a thick, soft, spreadable, sugar-based mixture used to fill and decorate baked goods. (The entry for "frosting" in *Merriam-Webster* is literally "icing," which is decidedly unhelpful.)

But according to experts I consulted, frosting and icing are, in fact, different. "Frosting would be something spreadable that you would apply and make swoopy," says cookbook author Erin McDowell. "Icing is something you would spoon or pour, though it might set to be as firm as frosting eventually." (This brings to mind royal icing, which is certainly thinner than buttercream.) The actual baked good in question can also affect the wording: "I wouldn't say that I 'frosted' cinnamon buns; I would say I 'iced' the cinnamon buns," says McDowell. "Even if what I was putting on them was cream-cheese frosting."

Yes, I find this as maddening as you do.

Luckily, **glaze** is distinct enough to be in its own category. It's thinner than frosting and icing, liquidy enough to be poured over the top of something and drip down the sides. When dry, it hardens into a shiny, smooth surface, giving whatever it anoints a healthy sheen. Confectioners' sugar (page 191) is often used in glazes: its granules are small enough to dissolve easily, and the cornstarch gives it a glossy glow.

Ginger Ale vs. Ginger Beer

If you've ever gotten the spicy kick of **ginger beer**, whether in a Moscow mule or a dark 'n' stormy or just slugged back on its own, you know it's a far cry from the stuff from a vending machine that you sip when you have a stomachache. But what makes it different?

Ginger beer comes from nineteenth-century England, a concoction of ginger, sugar, water, and sometimes lemon that was fermented with a starter culture called "ginger beer plant." Back then, the beverage had around 11 percent alcohol, but today, most ginger beers contain less than 0.5 percent or none whatsoever. Some are brewed with champagne yeast (page 203), while others are made bubbly by injecting carbon dioxide into the liquid.

Ginger ale was invented around a hundred years later, by a doctor named C. R. May in South Carolina; according to *The Cook's Essential Kitchen Dictionary*, he added Jamaican ginger to the local, mineral-rich well water to make it more palatable for his patients. These days, ginger ale is really just a ginger-flavored soft drink—no brewing or fermentation involved. It's lighter in color and much sweeter than ginger beer, without the richness and potency that makes the latter so memorable. (It does, however, pair well with Saltines.)

Green Tea vs. Matcha

Before we get into specifics, let's start with this truly mind-blowing fact: ALL TEA COMES FROM THE SAME PLANT. Earl Grey, Assam, jasmine, sencha, plain old Lipton—all *Camellia sinensis*. The differences between the teas lie in the treatment, processing, and fermentation of the leaves.

When you steam, roll, and dry the leaves in such a way that they keep their verdant color, you get **green tea**. Since there's no fermentation involved, they retain a pleasantly grassy, slightly bitter flavor, different from robust, aromatic black teas.

Matcha is a type of green tea, one so revered in Japan that tea ceremonies were built around it in the twelfth century. (If you think it's just trendy now, you're a few hundred years behind.) To make matcha, tea bushes are shaded from direct sunlight for twenty days before harvest, which jacks up their chlorophyll levels and increases production of the amino acid L-theanine, a compound that gives us a sense of calm. Once the best leaves are handpicked, they're steamed and either laid out to dry as is or rolled out beforehand. The rolled-out leaves become a fancy green tea named *gyokuro*, and the non-rolled-out leaves, called *tencha*, are stripped of stems and veins and stone-ground into what we know as matcha.

When it's time for a mug, the powder gets whisked into water using a special bamboo brush, creating a suspension and turning the liquid into an airy, sippable froth. The result is grassy and vegetal, with a hint of sweetness, like drinking a pure bowl of the color green. And since you're not just steeping the leaves and removing them—like classic green tea—you're consuming what amounts to a powdered salad, and therefore getting more vitamins, antioxidants, and caffeine.

There are many grades and distinctions between types of matcha, but the two to know are **ceremonial** and **culinary grade**. Ceremonial matcha is the stuff you want to drink on its own, whether whisked into water or into hot milk for a latte. Culinary grade, which is less expensive, is better for baking or making smoothies—scenarios where you're looking for that pop of color or a boost of vitamins and don't need the product to shine on its own.

Grinder vs. Hero vs. Hoagie vs. Sub

Some things in life are simple: we know that two pieces of bread with stuff between them, for example, is a sandwich. Swap in a long roll, however, and things get a lot more complicated.

Let's start with the **submarine**, or **sub**. A sub is at least six inches long and is constructed with a combination of meat, cheese, fixings (lettuce, tomato, etc.), and dressing. It is usually served cold. According to Google Trends, the word "sub" is by far and away the most commonly used term in every state . . . besides Pennsylvania.

That's because Pennsylvanians have their "**hoagies**." A hoagie is just a sub—the *Oxford English Dictionary* literally defines it as a "submarine sandwich"—but Pennsylvania folk have insisted on making it their own. According to *Bon Appétit,* the term likely comes from Depression-era jazz musician and sandwich-shop owner Al De Palma, who started calling his submarines "hoggies" because you "had to be a hog" to eat a sandwich that big. (So judgy!) "Hoggies" somehow morphed into "hoagies," and a regional sandwich term was born.

Head over to New York City, and you'll see a similar sandwich referred to as a "**hero**." The term likely comes from *New York Herald Tribune* columnist Clementine Paddleford, who in 1936 described a sandwich so large "you had to be a hero to eat it." A hero can refer to both hot and cold sandwiches, which is why you'll see things like meatball heroes and chicken-parm heroes on menus around the area.

Lastly, we have **grinders**, which is the New England–based term for a hero. According to *Bon Appétit,* some claim the sandwich was named for dockworkers—"grinders" in Italian-American slang—who would grind and sand the rusty hulls of boats to repaint them. But the term most likely comes from the fact that they were harder to chew than normal sandwiches: "That toothsomeness got translated into 'grinder,' since that's what your teeth had to do to get through a bite."

Hash Browns vs. Home Fries

Hash browns are made from potatoes that have been par-cooked in some way, whether it's boiling, steaming, or microwaving; mixed with any additional ingredients to form a homogenous mixture; and fried into a crisp, golden cake/patty/squashed-looking thing with frazzled edges. That potato mass can be shaped or shapeless, medusa-like or tidy, but the key is its shredded-but-still-held-together-ness.

Home fries are simply potatoes that are chopped, sliced, or diced and then fried. They're often parboiled first, which helps achieve the ideal home-fry texture: fluffy interior, crunchy exterior. Sliced onions and/or peppers sometimes join the party. What's key about home fries is that the pieces of potato—whether they're in half-moons or cubes—are distinct from one another, rather than a shaggy mass.

Some more fried-potato facts:

- Waffle House serves 238 hash-brown orders a minute.

- According to the book *Menu Mystique*, the first recipe for rösti—the shredded-potato cake thought to be the predecessor to hash browns—was found in Switzerland in 1598.

- French fries first appeared in America in 1802, when Thomas Jefferson, the president at the time, had the White House chef serve "potatoes in the French style" (described as "potatoes deep-fried while raw, in small cuttings") at a state dinner.

- When McDonald's introduced their hash browns to the breakfast menu in 1977, their advertising read: "Hash Browns: A great taste in a funny shape." What was "funny" back then is now iconic, because who hasn't had that oval-shaped puck of absolute deliciousness and marveled at its ingenuity? Say what you want about McDonald's, but those hash browns are fire.

ICE CREAM

& FROZEN DESSERTS

Frozen Yogurt vs. Gelato vs. Ice Cream

Whether we're talking New York Super Fudge Chunk or Chocolate Peanut Butter Split or just plain, pure vanilla, there's a defining trait that unites all American **ice cream**: according to the FDA, each carton must contain at least 10 percent butterfat (fat from cream and milk). Standard or "Philadelphia-style" ice creams are made with cream, milk, sugar, and various other minor ingredients; French or custard ice creams have the addition of egg yolks. (That's why French vanilla is yellow.)

---

* Turns out the city of brotherly love was also once famed for its ice cream; according to James Beard in the *Los Angeles Times*, "iced creams"—a mixture of cream, sugar, and eggs beaten in metal bowls over ice—were served at presidential dinners to George Washington, back when Philadelphia was the seat of government. Now, Philadelphia-style ice cream is known for its *lack* of eggs, because sometimes history is weird like that.

Both types are served at around 0–10°F, which gives them a firm texture and makes for an arm workout for whoever is scooping it.

Gelato is required by Italian law to have 3.5 percent butterfat—significantly less than American ice cream. The more butterfat a mixture contains, the more air it's able to absorb while churning, so gelato contains significantly less air than ice cream—which makes it taste richer and more flavorful. It's also served at a warmer temperature—between 10 and 20°F—giving it a softer, glossier texture.

Frozen yogurt, which became popular in the seventies and eighties, also contains less butterfat than regular ice cream—the percentage depends on whether the product is "low-fat" or "non-fat." It's able to stay frozen thanks to various additives, such as corn syrup, powdered milk, or vegetable gums. But frozen yogurt barely contains any yogurt at all; according to Harold McGee's *On Food and Cooking*, the standard proportion of other dairy to yogurt is 4:1. And depending on the recipe, the yogurt bacteria cultures may be entirely eliminated during the process, depriving you of the good-gut benefits that comes along with them.

Float vs. Frappe vs. Malt vs. Milkshake

A **milkshake** is a blended concoction made with ice cream, milk, and sometimes flavored syrup. But in New England, what the rest of the country thinks of as a milkshake is actually called a **frappe** (pronounced "frap"), and what New Englanders think of as a milkshake is actually just frothed-up milk and syrup.

In more regional terms: people in certain parts of Rhode Island and Massachusetts call a frappe a "cabinet," and it's usually flavored with Autocrat coffee syrup. A cabinet is called a cabinet because that's . . . where . . . the blender is kept. Not a particularly creative name, if I'm being frank.

A **malt**, or "malted," is just a milkshake with malted-milk powder added, which gives it an extra *oomph* of milkiness and body. Malted-milk powder is made with a grain, usually barley, that's been sprouted, dried in a kiln, ground up finely, and mixed with wheat flour and powdered milk. It was originally meant to be a health supplement, but people liked the flavor, and it eventually became a soda-fountain staple.

And speaking of soda, a **float** is a glass of soda with a scoop or two of ice cream floating in it—a fizzy, sweet, half-melted, half-solid beverage-food that's best consumed with a spoon. Vanilla ice cream with root beer is a classic combo, but I have a dear friend who enjoys one with cookies 'n' cream and Sprite, and I will grudgingly say that it's delicious.

Sherbert vs. Sherbet vs. Sorbet

Sorbet is simply a mix of fruit, water, and sugar, which is then churned together like ice cream. **Sherbet** is sorbet with the addition of a bit of milk or cream; according to USDA regulations, it must contain 1–2 percent butterfat.

And **sherbet** vs. **sherbert**? They're actually the same thing. The word in question comes from the Arabic word *sharba*, which means "to drink"—which then got adapted into *şerbet* in Turkish and *sharbat* in Persian. When the word was imported into English in the early seventeenth century, the spelling was all over the place: "sherbet" and "sherbert" are the two variations that are still used today.

By the late eighteenth century, "sherbet" had become the established spelling, though "sherbert" staged a minor comeback in the twentieth century. Now, we're generally back to using "sherbet," though "sherbert" is still a fully established variant. (So if you, like me, grew up using that term, you're still correct!)

Kosher vs. Sea vs. Table Salts

Salt, as we learn in high school, is just NaCl: a compound made from numbers 11 and 17 on the periodic table, a material so simple that it's treated as the most basic example of how chemistry works. But in real life, salt can get complicated, making one wonder why teens are taught the molar mass of NaCl rather than the differences between the items in the grocery aisle.

Let's start with **table salt**. Table salt is made of small, cubic crystals usually mined from underground rock-salt deposits, not sea water. As much as 2 percent of its weight is made up of additives that keep the salt crystals from sticking together—such as silicon dioxide, which is used in glass and ceramics—and then more additives to keep those additives from sticking together. It's also the densest of the salts, which makes it the slowest to dissolve—and when it does dissolve, those additives can make something like a brine look and taste murky.

On the other side of the spectrum is **kosher salt**, which is more pure than the other salts on the market. Kosher salt can come from either salt mines or the sea, and it was originally used in the koshering process of meats; the salt would remove impurities and draw the blood out of whatever animal was meant to be koshered. Lots of cooks now use kosher salt in all kinds of cooking; its coarse, uniform texture makes it easy to grab, and at around $1 per pound, it's inexpensive.

A note about kosher salt: the two top brands on the market, Diamond Crystal and Morton, behave very differently. Morton is much denser than Diamond Crystal, and therefore a volume measurement (like, say, a tablespoon) will be "saltier." Morton also takes longer to dissolve, which makes it easier to over-salt a dish; if you try something right after salting it, it won't taste as salty as it will be when all the salt dissolves. When given the choice, many cooks typically prefer Diamond Crystal over Morton.

Moving on: **sea salts**, as their name implies, come from the sea; they're produced through the evaporation of sea water or water from saltwater lakes. They often contain natural minerals, like magnesium and calcium, as well as teensy bits of natural sediments that can affect their color: think **Himalayan pink salt** or French **sel gris**. The coarser the sea salt, the more irregular the granules become, which makes them better for garnish or texture than for day-to-day cooking.

If you're looking for even fancier crystals, there's **flake salt** and **fleur de sel**. Flake salt, like Maldon, comes in flat, extended shapes rather than granules; those flakes are created either through evaporation or by rolling out granulated salts by machine. And fleur de sel is made from the crystals that form on the sea-salt beds in central or western France when the humidity and breeze are just right; they're scooped off of the surface just before they have the chance to dunk beneath the water. Sounds like fancy salt production, yes, and like a dream vacation, too.

Lamb vs. Mutton

Who decided to make *Ovis aries* so confusing? Let's first define all the words used to describe the members of the species:

Lamb: A sheep that's under a year old as well as the meat of those animals.

Ram: A male sheep.

Ewe: A female sheep.

Hogget: The U.K. term for meat of a ram or ewe that's between 1 and 2 years old.

Mutton: In the U.S., the meat of a ram or ewe that's over 1 year old. In the U.K., the meat of a ram or ewe that's over 2 years old.

So when we talk about sheep in the context of food, we're working with three terms: **lamb, hogget,** and **mutton**. In the U.S., lambs are sold in a range of ages (from 1 to 12 months) and weights (20–100 pounds). Meat between 6 and 10 weeks old is sometimes called "baby lamb," and "spring lamb" is from sheep between 5 and 6 months.

As sheep get older, their meat gets tougher, redder, and fattier—and that fat, which is creamy and whitish-pinkish in lamb, gets harder and whiter. The flavor of the meat also gets stronger and gamier, making mutton particularly polarizing—at least here in the U.S. In France, the Caribbean, parts of Africa, the Middle East, parts of China, Australia, and New

Zealand, mutton is eaten widely, and though it fell out of favor in Britain after World War II, the Prince of Wales actually called it "my favorite dish." I personally am rooting for old lamb to have a moment, especially if it means we get to use the word "hogget" more often.

Liqueur vs. Liquor

Liquor is a generic term for any distilled alcoholic beverage—anything from vodka to tequila (page 151) to brandy (page 16) to whiskey (page 51). In short: it's booze.

But what does "distilled" actually mean? Distillation is the process of separating out the different components of a liquid by heating it to its boiling point, then collecting the vapor. That vapor is then cooled back into a liquid, which is now a purified and/or concentrated version of the original substance. The apparatus this process happens in is called a still.

There are two types of stills: pot stills and continuous stills. Pot stills consist of a copper or copper-lined pot with a rounded bottom and a long, tapering neck, which is connected with a copper pipe to a condenser (a cooled spiral tube). When a fermented liquid is brought to a boil in the pot, the vapor travels up into the condenser, which cools it down into a "distillate" with a higher alcohol concentration than the original substance. Sometimes, depending on the type of spirit, the liquid is passed through the still multiple times in order to achieve a desired ABV (alcohol by volume) and/or flavor profile; Cognac (page 16), for example, goes through twice, as does Scotch (page 51).

Continuous stills are made of straight columns (they're sometimes called "column stills"). The column is fitted with a series of trays, each one slightly cooler than the one beneath it. The fermented liquid you're distilling gets pumped into the column at around the halfway point and, thanks to gravity, drips down through the trays. At the same time, a blast of steam comes up through the bottom, causing the liquid to va-

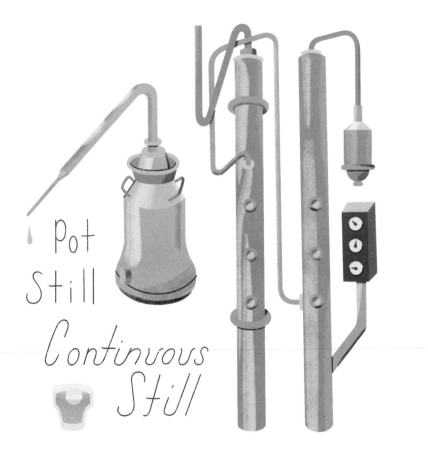

Pot
Still

Continuous
Still

porize. The vapor then travels up through the trays, constantly condensing and then vaporizing again, going from liquid to gas to liquid to gas. Each time that happens, some more of the impurities and heavier compounds are left behind, increasing the "purity" (and alcohol volume) of the spirit as it works its way up the column. When it reaches the desired specifications, the distiller draws off the vapor into a condenser, where it cools back into a liquid. Thanks to its constant flow of incoming material and outgoing product, the continuous still allows for a lot more stuff to be distilled at the same time, opening up opportunities for the kind of mass production that a pot still can't keep up with.

Liqueur is a specific type of liquor that's sweetened with sugar and flavored with fruit, herbs, spices, nuts, flowers, leaves, seeds, barks, or roots. Examples include Aperol, Cynar, and Campari (page 6), triple sec, Cointreau, amaretto, curaçao . . . the list goes on. According to Harold McGee's *On Food and Cooking*, alcohol's chemical makeup makes it a great solvent (i.e., a liquid that something gets dissolved into) for volatile, aromatic molecules; when solid ingredients are introduced into it, it can grab and hold onto their flavors. Most liqueurs are made with a neutral alcoholic base, but some use brandy or whiskey: Grand Marnier is Cognac and orange peel, for example, and Southern Comfort is bourbon with peach brandy and peaches.

The base spirit gets flavored through maceration, percolation, and/or distillation. Maceration is just a fancy word for infusion: the fruit, herbs, or whatever ingredients are simply soaked in the booze, then filtered out before bottling. With percolation, the ingredients are suspended in a narrow funnel and the alcohol is passed through it. And with distillation, the base spirit and additional ingredients go through the same process we just talked at length about above. According to *Meehan's*

Bartender Manual, distillation allows for the more controlled extraction of certain nuanced flavors, such as the citrusy notes of coriander seeds (page 98) or the herbal qualities of wormwood.

Liqueurs usually range from 15 to 40 percent ABV, and most contain a minimum of 100 grams of sugar per liter. A notable exception is crème de cassis, which has at least 400 grams per liter.

Lox vs. Nova vs. Smoked Salmon

There are two major processes in play when discussing the salmon you put on your bagel: **curing** and **smoking**. **Curing** happens when a food is preserved in salt, sometimes with additional flavorings or aromatics. **Smoking** involves exposing food to, well, smoke—with a "cold-smoke" for salmon happening below 85°F, and a "hot-smoke" for salmon happening above it. According to Niki Russ Federman, the co-owner of Russ & Daughters, "Cold-smoked salmon is the stuff that can be sliced so thin you can read the *Times* through it. Cured salmon has a similar texture, but without any smoke flavor. Hot-smoked salmon has a completely different texture—meaty and flaky, like cooked salmon."

Lox—or "belly lox," which is the actual name for it—is salmon that has been cured in salt. (Like **gravlax**, which is cured in sugar and salt, there's no smoking involved.) Lox is the type of preserved salmon people ate before refrigeration; salmon from the Pacific was hauled across the country in gigantic salt baths and fed to the Jewish immigrants of New York before *shul*. The taste of true lox is incredibly salty and assertive; "We think bagels with lox was invented because belly lox needed bread and dairy to cut it," says Niki. "People will constantly come in and ask for lox, and it sometimes requires a little back and forth to find out what they're actually looking for. Most people end up wanting smoked salmon."

To Niki, the "quintessential smoked salmon" is **Gaspe Nova**, or **Nova** for short. "Nova" refers to both the geographical location where the fish is caught (Nova Scotia) and the style of smoked salmon, in which the fish is first cured and then lightly smoked.

At Russ & Daughters, you'll find the luxe Gaspe Nova—with a "marbling and fattiness that give the salmon a silky quality"—along with Scottish salmon and Western Nova. Scottish salmon is a great middle ground: "It has a lovely smoke to it, but since it's a fat salmon, it retains a lot of moisture and silkiness," says Niki. Western Nova, which is made with wild king salmon, is leaner and more muscular, with a tighter texture and more assertive flavor than the other styles.

Rounding out the salmon options is **kippered salmon**, which is hot-smoked at 150°F. This gives it a texture more akin to poached salmon, and it's served in straight up-and-down slices rather than the paper-thin cuts of cold-smoked or cured stuff.

One more thing: don't call this stuff "deli." "In the Jewish tradition, you don't mix meat and dairy, so appetizing is fish and dairy—stuff you'd eat with bagels," says Niki. "It's the sister food tradition to deli"—which is the meat version of appetizing—"and it's been that way for over a hundred years."

Marmite vs. Vegemite

If you've only lived in the U.S., you'd be forgiven for not knowing what Marmite and Vegemite are, let alone the difference
between them. The two products look eerily similar—both outside and inside the jar—and are both made with a thick, dark
paste called yeast extract.

Yeast extract is a by-product of beer-making. Spent yeast
from a brewery gets mixed with salt and heated, which kicks off
a process called autolysis: enzymes break down the proteins,
nucleic acids, and carbohydrates in the yeast cells, resulting
in a goop that's filled with free glutamic acids, the compounds
behind umami. That goop is put through a centrifuge, which
separates the liquid (the good stuff) from the solid cell walls
(which get used in animal feed). Water is then evaporated out
of the liquid until it reaches the desired consistency, and then
the mixture is blended and flavored with vegetable extracts.
The result: a salty, savory, powerful paste that's usually spread
very, very thinly on toast.

If you're like, *What sick person decided to do all this when you could just put jam on toast instead?*, the answer is a man named Justus Freiherr von Liebig. The nineteenth-century German chemist figured out you could turn that beer-making waste into an edible product—a process then commercialized by the **Marmite Food Company** in 1902 in Burton-upon-Trent, England, two miles from the Bass brewery. Demand was so hot that in 1907, the company opened a factory in London and started shipping out a milder version to Australia and New Zealand. Once scientists realized that the product was particularly high in B vitamins, it became popular in schools and hospitals, and tons of it were shipped to British soldiers overseas in both world wars.

In 1919, after Marmite exports to Australia were disrupted by World War I, the food manufacturer Fred Walker & Co.—which would later become Kraft—tapped a Melbourne chemist named Cyril Percy Callister to develop a similar product named **Vegemite**. Like the Marmite folks, they used refuse from a brewery, blended with vegetable flavorings.

So now we have not one, but two iconic brands of yeast extract, born on different sides of the world, both of which happen to be packaged in glass jars with red-and-yellow labels. But how do the products themselves stack up? Vegemite is darker and thicker, with the texture of peanut butter; Marmite is thinner and runnier, more of a syrup than a paste. Vegemite is more intense too, with a brasher, saltier funk than its predecessor. The brand you're more devoted to most likely depends on where you're from—or, like me, you can just bow out of the debate altogether, and eat jam on toast instead.

Mezcal vs. Tequila

Tequila is a type of **mezcal**, just like Scotch is a type of whisky (page 51) and Cognac is a type of brandy (page 16). Here's how tequila differs from the rest of the mezcal family—and why the two terms are so confusing.

What They're Made From

Both mezcal and tequila come from the agave plant: a succulent with spiky leaves that looks like a cactus but is actually related to the asparagus. Mezcal can be made with over thirty varieties of agave, while tequila comes from just one: *Agave tequilana* Weber var. azul, also known as the blue Weber agave.

Where They're Made

Tequila is only permitted to be distilled in the Mexican states of Jalisco, Guanajuato, Tamaulipas, Nayarit, and Michoacán. And while mezcal refers to the entire category of agave spirits, the term is typically reserved for the specimens produced in Oaxaca and eight other states in Mexico.

How They're Made

Though you may be distracted by the agave plant's spikes— some can grow to up to nine feet long—the part that actually matters for production is the core of the stem, the *piña*. Once the piña is harvested, it's cooked to soften up its fibers and to convert its starches into sugar. For tequila, the piña is steamed in ovens; for mezcal, it's roasted in underground pits, which are lined with hot rocks and covered with straw mats. The cooked plant then gets pulverized, either by machine, machete, or *ta-*

hona, a giant stone wheel drawn by a mule or donkey. The resulting pulp is fermented with either wild or cultivated yeast and then distilled. From there, the spirit goes is aged in barrels or goes straight to bottling.

What They Taste Like

The most defining characteristic of mezcal is its smokiness, which it gets from its sizzle session underground. Beyond that, it's hard to pin down exact adjectives to differentiate one category from the other. As John deBary writes in *Drink What You Want*, there's huge variation within just the tequila category; like wine, the growing conditions of the plant have an important effect on the finished product. It can be sweet and light and fruity, earthy and mineral-y, nutty and sweet-potato-y, and more.

How They're Labeled

Both tequila and mezcal are labeled by the amount of time they've spent in the barrel. Older spirits are more caramelly in both flavor and color, picking up hints of whatever wood they're aged in.

For tequila:

Blanco or silver: aged 0–2 months
Reposado: aged from 3 months to 1 year
Añejo: aged 1–3 years
Super añejo: aged more than 3 years

For mezcal:

Joven: aged 0–2 months
Reposado: aged from 3 months to 1 year
Añejo: aged at least 1 year

Fettuccine vs. Linguine vs. Pappardelle vs. Tagliatelle

Italians may be known as laid-back, easygoing folk, the kinds of people who take afternoon siestas and the month of August for vacation. But that attitude does not apply to the world of pasta, where definitions can be unforgivingly strict and hyper-specific from region to region.

Take **tagliatelle**, for example. Like fettuccine, linguine, and pappardelle, tagliatelle is a long, flat noodle. The name comes from the verb *tagliare*, which means "to cut," and it's made by cutting a flour-and-egg dough into thin strips. (Factory-made versions are sometimes made with flour and water and are sold in nests.) In 1972, members of the Bologna delegation of the Accademia Italiana della Cucina went down to the city notary and officially registered the dimensions of an authentic *tagliatelle Bolognese*: cooked and served, it must measure exactly eight millimeters wide. A golden tagliatelle of regulation size is actually available at the local chamber of commerce, in case you're in the area and want to check out a visual.

Unlike the more location-specific pastas, tagliatelle can be found all around Italy and is usually served with regional sauces: *al ragù* in Emilia-Romagna, for example, or *al tartufo bianco* in Umbria.

Fettuccine is made with flour, eggs, and sometimes a bit of water. Like tagliatelle, it's cut from a sheet of dough; the name means "little ribbons." It's typically two to three millimeters wider than tagliatelle and around double the thickness, but in central and southern Italy (cover your ears, Bologna) they're often synonyms for each other. You may also see fettuccine made with alternative flours, such as chestnut flour in the mountainous regions. For serving, fettuccine is often tossed with a meat ragù, then topped with grated cheese.

Pappardelle is made in the same fashion as tagliatelle and fettuccine, though the thickness and shape of the pasta varies from region to region. The name is a term in the Tuscan dialect that comes from *pappare*, or "to eat." Though you'll now see it all over Italy, pappardelle's home base is northern and central Italy, especially Emilia-Romagna, Tuscany, the Marche, and

Umbria. Like fettuccine, it's often served with a meaty ragù, especially one made with game.

Linguine, which means "little tongues," is shaped like tagliatelle but is produced in a factory, not by hand. It's made with durum-wheat flour and water—no eggs—and is sold in flat boxes rather than in nests. You'll find linguine all over Italy, served with a variety of regional sauces, but the most famous dish is in Liguria, sauced with pesto Genovese.

Penne vs. Rigatoni vs. Ziti

Let's start with what makes these pasta shapes confusing: penne, ziti, and rigatoni are all hollow, cylindrical pastas made using the extrusion process, where the dough is forced through a die into the desired shape. They're all made with just durum wheat and water. Their large surface areas are wonderful transportation vessels for both meaty sauces and simpler ones. And, like all pastas, they are very good to eat.

As for the differences, it's time to get out some graph paper. Here are the exact dimensions, according to *The Geometry of Pasta*, and what makes the shapes unique.

Penne
Length: 2.12 inches
Width: 0.4 inches
Wall thickness: 1 mm

"Penne" comes from the Italian word for "quill," and if you take a thoughtful look at it, it's not hard to see why: the pasta, like its namesake, has its ends cut at an angle, gifting it with a large surface area for sauce to be drawn into the tubes. Penne can be smooth (*lisce*) or ridged (*rigate*), with the ridged ones being a bit sturdier and more soak-up-the-sauce-able than their smoother siblings.

Ziti
Length: 2 inches
Width: 0.4 inches
Wall thickness: 1.25 mm

Penne

Ziti

Rigatoni

A whopping 0.12 inches shorter and 0.25 millimeters thicker than penne, ziti is a smooth-exteriored pasta that hails from Naples, Italy. Notably, its ends are cut straight rather than at a diagonal, making it possible to distinguish it from penne without pulling out a ruler. The word "ziti" comes from the word for "bridegroom" or "the betrothed," and it's traditionally served as the first course of a wedding lunch. It's closely related to *ziti candele* (also known as just *candele*), another type of pasta that's twice the width and three times the length and needs to be broken up into pieces before cooking so it can fit into a pot.

Rigatoni
Length: 1.8 inches
Width: 0.6 inches
Wall thickness: 1 mm

Slightly shorter and wider than ziti and penne, rigatoni can be straight or slightly curved, depending on the extrusion process. It's always ridged, with square-cut ends similar to ziti. "Rigatoni" comes from the Italian word *rigare*, which means "to furrow" or "to rule"—and its ridges give a sauce plenty of area to furrow into. Also: rigatoni rules!

PICKLES

Brining vs. Curing vs. Marinating vs. Pickling

Before there were CBD seltzers and cauliflower pizza crusts and tie-dye Frappuccinos and zoodles, and even before things like refrigerators and chest freezers and ice boxes, humans had to eat. And surrounded by meats and fish and fruits and vegetables and other delicious stuff that gets decidedly undelicious after time in the hot sun, our ancestors had to get creative. They had to figure out how to preserve those precious goods: to keep them fresher for longer, to make them taste good even after hanging out for days or weeks or months or years. They started pickling, brining, marinating, and curing—methods that we still use today, even if we don't always understand the differences between them.

But before we start stocking our pantries, we need to talk about salt and acid. Salt and acid are the two major mediums in which food can be preserved; they're the things that keep it from spoiling, and in many cases, the things that transform the food into something wholly new. When we talk about preserving (and/or flavoring) with salt, we're talking about **brining**;

when we talk about preserving (and/or flavoring) with acid, we're talking about **marinating**.

A classic **brine** is a mixture of salt and water, and it can be used to preserve and/or flavor pretty much anything: vegetables, fruits, meats, fish. (You may also see foods "dry-brined," which means they're covered in salt, not immersed in salt water.) Brining meat for a few hours or days before cooking it makes for a juicier and more tender final product; the salt disrupts the structure of the muscle filaments, allowing the meat to absorb more liquid and helping to prevent it from getting too tough. Brining fish for a short period of time has a similar effect, but you'll also see fish brined for much longer: stuff like lox (page 147), anchovies, and salt cod are brined for weeks or months. In those cases, the salt transforms the fish into entirely new ingredients; the salt inhibits the bad bacteria from proliferating and aids in the proliferation of new savory compounds, creating more complex flavors and aromatics where there were none before.

A **marinade**, on the other hand, relies on acid to do its job. Acids—such as vinegar, wine, fruit juices, and buttermilk—are great at killing microbes, making marination another great form of preservation. Marinades, like brines, also provide flavor, and like their salty cousins, they weaken a piece of fish or meat's muscle tissue and allow it to retain more moisture when cooked.

So where does **pickling** come into this? According to food scientist Harold McGee, a pickle is a food preserved through immersion in a brine (as in brining) or a strong acid (as in marinating). So: pickles can be brined, or marinated, or both! In order to be considered a pickle, however, the food must be *preserved* through either method, not just flavored; a steak that's marinated just before grilling isn't a pickle, for example. Though you'll sometimes see it in other contexts, the term "pickling" is most often used to refer to preserved vegetables and fruits: think bread 'n' butter pickles, olives, preserved lemons, kimchi, and sauerkraut, to name a few.

But when it comes to pickling, salt and acid (usually vinegar) have very different uses. Pickles that are brined, such as the aforementioned sauerkraut, kimchi, and preserved lemons, are also **fermented**; the salt encourages certain good microbes to flourish while preventing the growth of other microbes that cause the food to go bad. The characteristics of the pickle depend on the salt concentration, fermentation length, and temperature—as well as the actual thing being pickled, of course.

Pickles that are dunked in acid, on the other hand, are **unfermented**; the vinegar stops the growth of the spoilage-causing microbes and helps to flavor whatever is being pickled, but it doesn't stimulate the microbe growth that causes food to ferment. Pickling in acid is a lot faster and gives you more control over the texture of the final product, but the flavor that develops is less complex.

And what about **curing**? Curing refers to any way of preserving food and preventing spoilage: it can mean brining, pickling, marinating, or smoking. If you're doing something to food in order to make it last longer—short of, like, hiding a package of Oreos in the back of your pantry so that they're out of your line of sight—you're curing it.

Bread 'n' Butter vs. Kosher Pickles

Now that we know that pickles can be preserved in salt, acid, or both, we can start talking specifics.

Kosher pickles are cucumbers that are soaked in brine and left to ferment, usually in large barrels or vats. The longer the fermentation, the more sour the pickle: after one to two weeks, the cucumbers are "half sours," and after three months, they're "full sours." For **"kosher dills,"** the cucumbers are washed after fermentation and then put into a jar with more salt brine, garlic, and dill; to be **"genuine,"** the pickles must be flavored with garlic. Traditional koshers don't include vinegar in the brine, but a lot of the grocery-store versions nowadays will have it as an ingredient to keep the cukes shelf-stable.

Bread 'n' butter pickles are soaked in vinegar, brown sugar or sugar syrup, and aromatics like turmeric and ginger, giving the cucumbers a sweet-sour flavor and a yellowish, sometimes neon-looking hue. The name supposedly originated during the Great Depression, when pickles were a filling for a sandwich with bread and butter. Whether that's true or not—and research into recipes of the time makes the claim rather questionable—they're delicious between slices of bread, whether they're cold-cutted, hamburgered, or even peanut-buttered.

Cornichon vs. Gherkin

If you've worked your way through a meat-and-cheese board, you're likely familiar with the tart, mighty cornichon. Or are those cute little guys gherkins? Are they the same thing?

A **gherkin** is a species in the cucumber family called *Cucumis anguria*. They're smaller than standard cucumbers—around the size of your pinky finger and are picked when they're young; as they age, the pimply bumps on their surfaces become sharp spikes.

The term **"gherkin"** also refers to pickled versions of these cucumbers. They're soaked in a vinegar brine, often with sugar and spices like turmeric and celery seed. **Cornichons** are also pickled gherkins, but with a different flavor profile—the brine always includes tarragon, and there's no sugar in the mix.

Pie vs. Tart

Here's what pies and tarts have in common: They are baked things with crust and filling. They can be savory or sweet. They are delicious things to eat.

But there are marked differences between the two. **Pies** can have crust on the bottom, on the top, or on both the bottom and top; banana cream pie, double-crusted apple pie, lattice-topped pumpkin pie, and chicken pot pie are all, as their names suggest, pies. They generally have more filling than tarts do, and often have sides that angle outwards—though you can bake them in springform or straight-sided pans and be A-OK. And all pies—or the good ones, at least—should have a crispy, flaky crust, one that shatters when you fork into it and leaves a trail of fine, golden crumbs.

Tarts, on the other hand, have only a bottom crust, one that is denser and crumblier than that of a pie. Their sides are usually shallower, and they have less filling than pies do. Tarts are typically baked in a pan with a removable bottom, or in a pastry ring that gets unmolded before serving; they're therefore seen as less rustic than pies. And though tart fillings can run the gamut, you're likely to see them filled with stuff that's unbaked—think French pastry cream topped with fresh fruit, or layers of caramel and ganache—or lightly baked custards, like Portuguese *pastéis de nata*.

That's all nice and clear and satisfying, until you whisper to yourself: *Is a cheesecake a cake, pie, or tart?* You'll find the answer on page 112.

Pie

↓

↑

Tart

Baby Back Ribs
vs. Spareribs

When we're pawing into a rack of ribs, it's easy to think of them as being disembodied from the pigs themselves, perfectly butchered and portioned somewhere outside of our conscious ness and simply appearing, grilled/smoked/barbecued and sauced, on a platter in front of us.

Here's the reality: pigs are animals, and they have ribs. These ribs, when divided horizontally, are made up of two types of cuts: baby back ribs and spareribs.

Baby back ribs come from the parts of the ribs that are connected to the backbone, beneath the loin muscle, and are curved where they meet the spine. They're called "babies" be-cause they're shorter than spareribs; on the longest end, they're around six inches, and they taper down to about three inches on the shorter end. Depending on how they're butchered, they may have around a half-inch of loin meat attached to the top. Baby back ribs are more tender and leaner than spareribs, and are typically more expensive. Each rack is around two pounds,

about half of which is bone, and one rack feeds around one hungry adult.

Spareribs are cut from the ends of baby back ribs and run to the pig's breastbone. One side has exposed bone—that's where they meet the baby backs—and the other side, the side near the breastbone, is where the rib tips are, a flap of meat that has some small bones and cartilage in it. (**St. Louis–cut ribs** are spareribs with the rib tips removed.) Compared to baby backs, spareribs have more meat between the bones and less meat on top, and that meat generally has more marbling and flavor. The bones are straighter, longer, and flatter than baby backs, and a rack—which ranges from 2.5 to 3.5 pounds, around half of which is bone and cartilage—typically feeds two adults.

And **riblets**? True riblets are made by cutting a rack of ribs into two- to four-inch pieces. However, what Applebee's refers to as "riblets" are "button ribs," which are actually not ribs at all. They're from a long, thin cut of meat that runs along the spine just after the rearmost rib, a cut that's around 6 inches long, 1 1/2 inches wide, and 1/4 inch thick. There are no real ribs in there, just little round nubs (or "buttons") of bone to gnaw around.

Bacon vs. Pancetta vs. Guanciale

Bacon and pancetta are both made from pork belly—the differences are in how they're prepared and preserved.

For **bacon,** pork belly is cured (page 159) in a dry or wet brine and then cold-smoked. It comes in straight slices (unless it's slab bacon, which is a slab) and has less salt than pancetta or guanciale.

Pancetta is made by curing pork belly with salt, pepper, and sometimes other spices. It is not smoked. Pancetta usually comes in two forms: *arrolata,* in which the belly is rolled into a tight log, or *tesa,* where the belly comes in straight slices. You might also find it in pre-chopped hunks. In a pinch, bacon can be substituted for it in most dishes, though you'll probably want to blanch it first to tone down its smoky flavor.

Guanciale is another cured pork product, but it comes from the jowl rather than the belly. It gets rubbed with salt, pepper, and sometimes additional seasonings and is aged for at least three months. The result is even fattier than bacon and pancetta and adds a ton of flavor to a dish. It's most famously used in the classic Roman pasta dishes *amatriciana* (with tomato, onion, and red chile flakes), *carbonara* (with eggs and/or egg yolks, black pepper, and pecorino), and *gricia* (with just black pepper and pecorino).

Boar vs. Hog vs. Pig vs. Swine

In America, home of bacon-wrapped hot dogs and Smithfield ham and uncountable variations of barbecue (page 28), we have many names for porcine creatures: pigs, boars, hogs, sows, swine. They're in our farms and our forests, on our menus and our plates, but what differentiates one from the other?

All are part of the *Sus scrofa* species, which was first domesticated nine thousand years ago and brought to the Americas by Christopher Columbus. **"Swine"** is the most general term of the bunch, and it encompasses all of *Sus scrofa*: domesticated, wild, and feral; small and large; male and female.

In the U.S., the word **"pig"** refers to young, domesticated swine that weigh less than 180 pounds; anything larger is called a **"hog."** **Boars** are male swine that haven't been castrated, and **sows** are females that have reached adulthood.

But not all of *Sus scrofa* is domesticated; there are also wild and feral specimens, millions of which roam the U.S. and Canada. "Feral" swine have roots that can be traced back to escaped domestic pigs, while "wild" refers to any animal that's not domesticated. (Few purebred Eurasian wild boars, which were brought to Texas in the 1930s and released for hunting, still exist today, but they've bred with feral hogs.)

Feral/wild swine are thinner than their domesticated counterparts, with thicker hides of coarse, bristly hair. They develop smaller, narrower skulls with more defined snouts, rather than the rounder skulls of their kept brethren. Their tusks—which get cut from domestic pigs when they're born—are long and rounded, and they use them both as a defensive weapon and to forage for food. They can vary in color and coat pattern, but those that are dark-skinned are more likely to survive in the wild and pass along their genes. Boars that make it to breeding age develop muscular "shields" around their shoulders that grow harder and thicker as they get older; these protect them during fights.

Here are some more facts about feral swine:

- They're considered one of the most destructive invasive species in the United States. They breed rapidly, have no natural predators, and eat almost anything.

- They can be found in at least thirty-nine states and four Canadian provinces. In Texas alone, they cause at least $400 million of damage each year.

- Their tusks are actually teeth, and constant grinding keeps them super-sharp.

- They usually travel in groups called sounders, composed of two or three adult sows and their young. A sounder can be anywhere from four to fifty individuals. Boars usually live alone or in groups of bachelors, only joining sounders in order to breed.

Picnic vs. Pork Butt vs. Pork Shoulder

When butchers break down animals, they first separate them into primal cuts: large, heavy hunks of meat that then get portioned into more consumer-friendly sections. **Pork shoulder** is one of those primal cuts, along with the loin, belly, and hind leg. But when you say you're cooking pork shoulder, you're probably not cooking a twenty-pound hunk of meat—you're more likely cooking one of the shoulder's two sub-primal cuts, the **picnic shoulder** or the **pork butt**.

The **pork butt**, also known as a Boston butt, is higher on the pig's foreleg, directly behind its neck and head. It's a rectangular-shaped, well-marbled cut that's more tender than the picnic shoulder, since the muscle isn't used frequently. You can find it both bone-in and boneless at a butcher, and you'll often see it sold with the fat cap intact.

The **picnic shoulder** comes from lower down on the pig's foreleg. Since the muscle gets a lot of use, it's tougher than pork butt and has less intramuscular fat and marbling. The shape is more of a tapered triangle than a uniform rectangle, and it's frequently sold with the skin on.

When it comes to preparing them, both cuts lend themselves well to long-cooking methods like stewing, braising, and smoking. Pork butt is great if you're looking for even hunks of meat, since it's more regularly sized. And if you want some textural contrast, go for the picnic shoulder; since it's sold with the skin on, you'll get some crispy action too.

Prawns vs. Shrimp

There are few crustaceans as misunderstood as the shrimp and the prawn. Some people think they're the same thing; others think they differ only by size; others think they're simply called different things in different countries, or regions, or states. And yet: all of these people are wrong! Shrimp and prawns are completely different creatures. Shrimp belong to the suborder Pleocyemata, and prawns belong to the suborder Dendrobranchiata. Let's explore what that actually means.

Gills: As you may remember from ninth-grade biology, gills are structured in a way that maximizes their surface area. Shrimp have plate-like gills, which consist of flat, layered arrangements; prawns have branching gills, which is where I'm assuming the "branchiata" part of Dendrobranchiata comes from.

Claws and Pincers: Shrimp have claws on two pairs of their legs, and their front pincers are the largest. Prawns have claws on three pairs of their legs, and their second pincers are larger than their front ones.

Body Structure: Both shrimp and prawns are decapods, which mean they have external skeletons and ten legs. You can divide a decapod into four major sections: the head, the thorax (the area right behind the head), the abdomen (the "torso"), and the tail. In prawns, the head overlaps with the thorax, which overlaps with the abdomen—much like shingles on a roof. In shrimp, the thorax overlaps with both the head and the abdomen, like a cummerbund.

Habitat: Prawns live in fresh water, while shrimp can come from either fresh water or salt water (though the majority of species come from salt water). Fun fact: the colder the water the shrimp is from, the smaller the size! (I always wondered why the shrimp in Scandinavian shrimp salads were so tiny, and now I have my answer.)

Size: Generally speaking, prawns are larger than shrimp—though this depends on the species.

Taste: Anyone who tries to tell you that shrimp and prawns taste different is wrong. Sure, some prawns are sweeter than shrimp, and vice versa—but the flavor is more dependent on the species, rather than the suborders as a whole.

Rhum vs. Rum

Rum is an umbrella term for sugarcane-based spirits: it can come from molasses, fresh-pressed sugarcane juice, or sugarcane syrup. According to *Meehan's Bartender Manual*, it's one of the most diverse categories of spirits: "It can be clear, amber-hued, or black, and its flavor spectrum ranges from nearly neutral to heady, high-proof drams." You'll find some version of rum in pretty much every tropical and subtropical sugarcane-growing country in the world.

Rhum is short for **rhum agricole**, a type of rum produced from sugarcane grown in one of the twenty-three designated municipalities on the French island of Martinique. It's known for its light, funky, almost vegetal flavor, with less sweetness than many other types of rum. To make it, fresh-pressed sugarcane juice—no syrup or molasses allowed—is fermented with indigenous yeast and distilled in a column still. The resulting spirit is 65–75 percent ABV when it heads into oak barrels for aging, and it gets diluted to 40 percent ABV before bottling.

Rhum blanc gets three months in the barrel; light-amber *rhum paille* is aged for no less than a year, and *rhum vieux* hangs out for a minimum of three years in barrels no larger than 650 liters.

Some more fun facts about rum:

- According to *Meehan's Bartender Manual*, rhum agricole became a thing during the Napoleonic Wars of the early nineteenth century, when government-subsidized beet sugar took the place of sugarcane sugar in France. That left many producers in Martinique with no market for their sugar and less molasses to make rum with. They decided to make rum from fresh sugarcane juice instead, and here we are today.

- The color of rum actually tells you very little about its age. Caramel color is added to both young rums and mature rums; the latter relies on it for a consistent look from batch to batch. On the other hand, white rums are actually barrel-aged to add flavor, then filtered with active charcoal to render them colorless.

- The first North American rum distillery was established in 1664 on what is now Staten Island, New York. Hardly a tropical locale.

Arborio vs. Bomba vs. Carnaroli Rice

If you've ever cooked risotto or paella, you know the type of rice is particularly important: for risotto, you need a type that will thicken and creamify the dish, and for paella, you need grains that absorb a ton of flavorful liquid while still retaining their texture.

Bomba rice is often called for in paella, since it can absorb lots of liquid—three cups of liquid to one cup of rice, in fact—without getting too sticky. Bomba and its cousin, **Calasparra rice**, are grown around the Spanish town of Calasparra in the southeastern part of the country.

For risotto, you need a rice that will slink off its starch into the liquid you're cooking with, giving the final dish heft and body. Arborio and carnaroli rice are your best bets. **Arborio** used to be grown exclusively in Italy, but it's now grown in the U.S. as well. It checks all the boxes you need for a risotto: medium-grain, starchy, high absorption rate. **Carnaroli** has a higher starch content and firmer texture than arborio, and it produces a creamier risotto that's harder to overcook. Other risotto-friendly rices you may come across are **vialone nano**, **baldo**, and **CalRiso**.

Of all the rice types we just talked about, **arborio** is the most common—you can find it at many American grocery stores. So can you use it for paella in a pinch? The answer is yes, but you'll need to tone down the liquid. It's not as absorbent as the Spanish varieties.

Fun fact: when you order risotto at a restaurant, the cook isn't starting the dish from scratch, pausing everything they're doing to sweat over the stove. Risotto actually lends itself well to being made in advance: cook it until it's just short of being done, and then pop it in the fridge. The cooling period allows some of the cooked starch to firm up, making the grains more resilient than if they had been cooked to completion. Then, when the time comes, just reheat the rice in a pan and finish it with more hot broth before serving.

Basmati vs. Jasmine Rice

Basmati and **jasmine rice** are types of long-grain rice that have unusually high amounts of volatile compounds, making them particularly aromatic.

But first, we need to talk about starch. Starch is made up of two compounds: amylopectin and amylose. Amylose is shaped like a straight line, while amylopectin has bushier branches. Many of rice's characteristics come from the ratio between these two molecules: varieties with more amylopectin are stickier when cooked, and amylose-y types are drier and firmer.

Basmati rice is popular on the Indian subcontinent and has a smell reminiscent of freshly popped popcorn. Thanks to its high amounts of amylose, the grains are flaky and distinct when cooked. There's a type of basmati called Texmati that's grown in the U.S., but the original variety is thought of as more fragrant.

Jasmine rice is grown primarily in Thailand and used in Southeast Asian cooking. The grains are a bit shorter and chubbier than basmati, though it's still considered long-grain. But unlike its long-grain cousins, jasmine rice has a lot of amylopectin, making it starchier, clumpier, and clingier to chopsticks. And though it shares basmati's popcorn scent, its aroma is actually a lot stronger, particularly when the rice is fresh.

Long-Grain vs. Medium-Grain vs. Short-Grain Rice

There are more than forty thousand varieties of rice around the world, and more than half of the people on this planet rely on it as a staple of their diets. You'll find it on tables from Japan to Argentina, Thailand to New York, and pretty much everywhere in between. But what exactly is it?

Rice is a grain, the small, edible seed of certain types of grass. It was cultivated three separate times, on three separate continents: *Oryza sativa*, the variants of which we eat by the bushel, was domesticated in China between 8,200 and 13,500 years ago. *Oryza glaberrima* was cultivated in Africa 2,000 to 3,000 years ago and is now only really grown for sustenance. The last type, once domesticated in Brazil, is no longer around—it was abandoned after European colonizers arrived.

There are two major subspecies of *Oryza sativa*: the **indica** rices, which have longer, thinner grains that are drier when cooked, and the **japonica** rices, which are shorter and stickier. Indica rices have a higher proportion of amylose, a starch compound that is straight and well-organized, and japonica varietals have more amylopectin, which has a bushy, branched shape.

Long-Grain Rice

Long-grain rice is around three to five times as long as it is wide. Basmati and jasmine (page 181) are two well-known examples. Most long-grain rice is of the indica variety, and thanks to the high proportion of amylose, their grains are dry and distinct when cooked. This makes them great for dishes like pilafs, biryani, and mujaddara.

Medium-Grain Rice

Medium-grain rice, usually of the japonica type, is stubbier and starchier than long-grain rice. It's around two to three times longer than it is wide. Generally speaking, medium-grain rice is fluffy when it's cooked and a bit clumpy as it cools, and it requires less water to cook than long-grain. It's the typical "table rice" in China, Japan, and Korea, and the type used to make risotto in Italy and paella in Spain.

Short-grain rice

Short-grain rice, also of the japonica subspecies, is starchier and stickier than long- and medium-grain rice. The grains are chubbier and rounder, only slightly longer than they are wide. These are the types like sushi rice and glutinous rice, which are easy to eat with chopsticks or your hands and remain tender at room temperature. You'll also find short-grain rice in desserts: coconut sticky rice in Southeast Asia, mochi in Japan, and rice pudding in America.

Russian vs. Thousand Island Dressing

If you've frequented a salad bar recently—or returned from a quick jaunt from, say, the 1950s—you may recall a vessel or two of pink, fluorescent dressing with some chopped-up stuff in it. Maybe you dolloped some of it onto your plate of greens or had anointed your sandwich with it. In any case: was it Russian dressing or Thousand Island? If it wasn't slapped in a bottle with a label, would you be able to tell the difference?

Russian dressing is made with a mayonnaise-ketchup base, often livened up with pickle relish, Worcestershire sauce, prepared horseradish, and lemon juice, and seasoned with paprika, onion powder, and/or mustard powder. It's spicier and less sweet than Thousand Island, with a more complex, nuanced je ne sais quoi. Some say it got the "Russian" in its name because it once contained caviar: according to a 1957 *New York Times* article, an early version of the dressing in *Larousse Gastronomique* called for mayonnaise, tinted pink with the poached coral and pulverized shell of a lobster, seasoned with black caviar and salt. In any case, the creator of the dressing, a man named James E. Colburn of Nashua, New Hampshire (not Russia), sold so much of it that he acquired "a wealth on which he was able to retire." Jealous.

Thousand Island dressing also has a mayonnaise-ketchup base, includes pickle relish and/or other chopped vegetables, such as pimientos, olives, and onions, and has some more rogue, recipe-dependent ingredients thrown into the mix, like parsley, chives, or hot sauce. The big differentiator is the addition of a chopped up hard-boiled egg, which acts as a thickener and binds the ingredients together. The name comes from the region between northern New York and southern Ontario, which is where it was invented around 1900—most likely at one of the resorts up there that city folk frequented in the summer.

These days, you're more likely to find the two dressings on sandwiches rather than salads: Russian on a Reuben, and Thousand Island-ish "secret sauce" on a Big Mac. But sadly, according to the *Washington Post*, "an examination of menus around the country shows that Russian dressing has all but disappeared from America's national consciousness." What's more, what is actually Russian dressing might now be labeled as Thousand Island. "Sometimes it's easier to just make things quickly understandable for the customer, to avoid wasting time explaining things," Nick Zukin, coauthor of *The Artisan Jewish Deli at Home*, told the *Post*. "Even if you made what was essentially a Russian dressing, you might call it Thousand Island just to avoid headaches."

Rutabaga vs. Turnip

Turnips, known as *Brassica rapa* in some circles, are edible roots that have been cultivated for four thousand years. Back in the ancient Roman times, according to *The Cook's Essential Kitchen Dictionary*, they were thought to help cure "the body's outer ills": the physician Dioscorides believed applying a fresh turnip to a sore foot would cure the pain immediately, and chef Apicius told women approaching middle age that rubbing a paste of cooked turnip, cream, and smashed rosebuds all over their face, neck, and shoulders would make their skin as soft and smooth "as a baby's thigh."

Turnips come in a number of shapes and colors, but they generally fall into two categories: Japanese and French. Japanese turnips, also known as Tokyo turnips, are round and white, while French turnips are more tapered at the bottom and have purple "shoulders," to borrow Alice Waters's delightful description from *Chez Panisse Vegetables*. Both types have stark-white flesh and leaves that grow directly attached to the top of the root. (The leaves make for good eating, too—if they come attached at the market, store them separately.) Turnips grow to around two to four inches in diameter but are best consumed when they're small and dainty. They're available throughout the year, with the sweetest and most tender ones harvested in the spring and fall.

Though they look the part, **rutabagas** are not just large yellow turnips; they're a species of their own, *Brassica napus*. The vegetable is the result of a turnip and a cabbage getting down and dirty and creating a whole line of progeny—proof that smelly, cruciferous vegetables know how to have a good time. The word "rutabaga" comes from its Swedish name *rotabagge*, which means "baggy root" (sexy) and explains why the plant is sometimes called a "swede." Rutabagas have yellow flesh and yellowish-purple skin, and their leaves grow around the neck of the root rather than out of the top. They're starchier and bigger than turnips, around six inches in diameter or larger, and are best harvested after a bout of cold weather, which helps coax out their sweetness.

Shoyu vs. Soy Sauce vs. Tamari

Soy sauce was first invented around two thousand years ago, using a process that is quite similar to the one used today. To make it, soybeans and roasted wheat are mixed together and inoculated with aspergillus mold, or *koji*. (Koji is also used for miso paste and sake.) After three to four days, the soybean-wheat-koji mixture is combined with water and salt to form a thick mash. The mash is put into large vats and fermented, traditionally for eighteen months or longer, and then strained and bottled.

Soy sauces can be **Chinese-style** or **Japanese-style**. Chinese-style soy sauces are traditionally made with 100 percent soy, while Japanese-style soy sauces are made with a mix of soy and wheat (usually 50/50). This gives the Japanese sauces a sweeter, more nuanced flavor than their Chinese counterparts, which can be saltier and more aggressive. **Shoyu** is simply the name for the Japanese-style soy sauce, which can be light (*usukuchi*) or dark (*koikuchi*).

Tamari is a soy-sauce-like product that originated as a byproduct of making miso. It's traditionally made with only soybeans and no wheat, giving it a flavor similar to Chinese-style soy sauce—and a great option for those who are gluten-free. Many tamaris these days, however, do contain a bit of wheat—so if you're concerned about gluten, make sure to check the bottle.

Other soy sauce variants include **Chinese light soy sauce**, or "fresh" or "thin" soy sauce, which is the most common soy sauce in Chinese cuisine; **Chinese dark soy sauce,** which is thicker, less salty, and sometimes contains sugar or molasses; and **sweet soy sauce,** or *kecap manis,* an Indonesian style popular across Southeast Asia. Sweet soy sauce is flavored with palm sugar, star anise, galangal, and other aromatics, giving it what writer Max Falkowitz calls a "barbecue-sauce consistency." It's popular in stir-fries as well as rice and noodle dishes, and it's also great in a marinade.

Before you buy any soy sauce or soy-sauce-like product, make sure to check the ingredients first. These days, there are bottles of stuff that are sold as soy sauce but contain chemicals aimed at replicating the soy sauce taste while bypassing the traditional fermentation process. According to Max, "If you see anything besides soybeans, wheat, salt, and mold cultures on the label, such as caramel coloring and 'natural flavors,' steer clear." With so many options on the shelves these days, it should hopefully be easy to do so.

Confectioners' vs. Powdered vs. Superfine Sugar

Superfine sugar (or **castor sugar**) is exactly what it sounds like: an extra-fine version of granulated sugar. That texture affects the structure of the baked goods it's in: when it's beaten with butter for cakes, for example, it's unable to create the same little air pockets that standard sugar does, giving the final product a denser, crumblier texture. A great use for it is in meringues, where the tiny crystals dissolve quickly and prevent the cookies from getting gritty or weepy. And bartenders love it for syrups and cold drinks: Ever add normal sugar to iced coffee and have it turn grainy? Superfine sugar won't do that.

Powdered or **confectioners' sugar** is sugar that's been ground so fine, it needs a bit of cornstarch mixed in (around 3 percent by weight) to prevent it from clumping. That starch works as a stabilizer in whatever dish it ends up in, helping to firm up whipped cream or a too-liquidy frosting in a pinch. It's particularly great for glazes (page 126): whisk it with a bit of liquid (like milk or water), and you'll get a thick, shiny, drizzle-able concoction that benefits a cake, or cookies, or really anything it anoints. Or just dust the top of a dessert with powdered sugar and call it a day—there's no easier way to make something feel fancy.

Make It Yourself!

For 1 cup of superfine sugar, process 1 cup plus 2 teaspoons of granulated sugar in a food processor or blender for 30 seconds.

For 1 cup of powdered sugar, process 1 cup of granulated sugar and 1 teaspoon of cornstarch in a food processor or blender for 1 minute, then pass through a fine-mesh strainer.

Light Brown vs. Dark Brown Sugar

What exactly is brown sugar, besides the stuff that spills everywhere when you try jamming a measuring cup into its mind-bogglingly narrow box and then, later, resembles a leaden brick that rivals a diamond in its impenetrability?* It's actually just white, refined sugar with the addition of molasses. The only differentiator between light brown and dark brown is the amount of those molasses: **light** has 3.5 percent, and **dark** has 6.5 percent.

Which raises the question: Can you swap one for the other? Turns out light and dark brown sugar are pretty much interchangeable. Dark brown sugar will give your final product a darker color and more robust flavor, but unless you're entering your baked good in a beauty contest, it doesn't really matter.

There's also a whole family of raw, unrefined brown sugars, which retain traces of minerals and acids from the sugarcane or palm-tree juice they come from. These are your **muscovado,**

---

* Here are some tips from around the internet for keeping brown sugar from hardening:

- Move the brown sugar into an airtight bag or container.

- Stick a piece of fresh bread in the container once you've opened it.

- Stick a marshmallow in the container once you've opened it.

- Stick a piece of apple in the container once you've opened it.

- Keep the brown sugar in the fridge or freezer.

turbinado, and **demerara** sugars, all of which have a more complex, nuanced flavor than the more processed varieties. You can use light or dark muscovado sugar as you would with standard light and brown sugar. The same can't be said for turbinado and demerara, which have larger, coarser crystals and make excellent crunchy toppings for muffins, pies, and quick breads.

Butterscotch vs. Caramel
vs. Cateja vs. Dulce de Leche

Caramel, butterscotch, dulce de leche, and cajeta: all sweet, golden, syrupy concoctions that harness the power of heat and sugar in different ways.

Caramel is made from slowly cooking granulated sugar, simply on its own or with a splash of water. As it melts and darkens, it breaks down into its component parts, which then react with each other to create complex, toasty flavors and aromas. The process starts at around 320°F, when the sugar melts into a liquid. At 340–350°F, you'll get a pale gold caramel, one that becomes brittle and glass-like as it cools: think of the stuff on the outside of a croquembouche. At 355–360°F, it'll turn medium-brown and will be not quite as hard when it sets. At 365–380°F, you'll get a deep amber caramel that becomes soft and sticky. The mixture will keep getting darker until it reaches 410°F, which is black-caramel territory. That stuff won't taste good and will likely ruin your pot, but it's used as a browning agent in manufacturing things like pumpernickel bread and cola.

Butterscotch is made from melting brown sugar with butter, and its flavor is sweeter and more rounded than that of caramel. It's wonderfully unscientific to make: just simmer the two things together until they thicken up a bit, and you're done.

Turns out brown sugar and butter are a powerful combo: the butter helps the sugar granules melt evenly, and the acid in the brown sugar's molasses keeps the mixture from crystallizing. You won't get the nuanced characteristics of caramel, but you'll have a delicious thing to eat in only a few, stress-free minutes.

Dulce de leche is made from slowly cooking cow's milk and sugar together, oftentimes for hours, into a rich, thick, spreadable dessert. Dulce de leche made with goat milk is known as **cajeta**. Both are cooked at a lower temperature than caramel—between 212°F and 220°F—and their golden color comes not from the caramelization of sugar, but from the browning of the lactose and lysine in the milk. Thanks to this technique, they have a more mellow, nutty, and complex taste than their cousins. Both dulce de leche and cajeta can also sometimes include baking soda, which balances out the pH of milk (which is slightly acidic) and speeds up the browning process.

So, in short:

granulated sugar (+ water)—> caramel

brown sugar + butter—> butterscotch

cow milk + sugar (+ baking soda)—> dulce de leche

goat milk + sugar (+ baking soda)—> cajeta

Sweet Potato vs. Yam

What if I told you that those candied "yams" you eat on Thanksgiving aren't actually yams? That the "yams" at the grocery store aren't either?

You, my friend, have been living a lie.

Those candied yams? Sweet potatoes. The grocery-store specimens? Sweet potatoes. Anything labeled "sweet potato"? Also probably sweet potatoes. (You'd think that'd be obvious, but who can trust anything anymore?)

The **sweet potato** is the root of the *Ipomoea batatas* plant, a member of the morning glory family. It is native to northern South America and has been cultivated since prehistoric times. The roots have a remarkably high sugar content—around 3–6 percent—that actually increases when they're stored at room temperature, and then again during the cooking process. There are a ton of different types: ones with deep-orange flesh, others that are how-can-this-be-found-in-nature purple, still others a pale yellow. You'll find two common varieties in the U.S.: the dark-orange type you eat on Thanksgiving, and ones with lighter-colored, drier, more crumbly insides.

Thanks to a 1930s marketing campaign, those dark-orange tubers started getting labeled as "**yams**." But yams they are not: true yams are a dozen or so different species from the *Dioscorea* genus, all related to tropical grasses and lilies. Yams come in all different shapes, sizes, and colors—their insides can be white, yellow, pink, or even dark brown—and they're generally starchier than sweet potatoes, with a creamier texture when cooked. Their name comes from "nyam," a West African term that means "to eat," and they're common in African, Caribbean, and South American cuisines. (In the U.S., you're most likely to encounter them in international or specialty markets.)

Some more fun facts about sweet potatoes and yams:

- Sweet potatoes were introduced to England via Spain as part of the dowry of Catherine of Aragon, the first wife of Henry VIII. He liked them so much, he was said to be able to eat twenty-four per meal. After his divorce from Catherine, he offered a prize of land and gold to the gardener who could successfully grow them in Britain.

- Hormones based on yam extracts are used to make birth control.

- Yams can grow to be over one hundred pounds, and in the Trobriands, a cluster of islands off the coast of Papua New Guinea, they've been honored with their own houses.

- Though the sweet potato was introduced to China relatively late in its history—in 1594, to be exact—China is now the largest grower of the tuber in the world, accounting for over half of sweet-potato output worldwide.

Summer Squash vs. Zucchini

All **summer squashes**—a category that includes zucchini as well as crookneck squash, pattypan squash, and various other varieties found at the farmers' market—are the immature fruit of the *Cucurbita pepo*, a species that includes winter squashes like delicata and acorn and even Halloween pumpkins.

Zucchini can be both green and yellow, though the green is more common outside of its summer season. Its shape is pretty much straight from top to bottom, with sometimes a slightly more bulbous end. Though zucchini as large as baseball bats are cool to look at, they're not the best for eating: the smaller ones will be more tender and less watery.

Yellow crookneck squash, the type you're most likely to confuse with zucchini, has more of a defined bulbous bottom and a tapered, curved neck. To get that curve, they're usually left to mature on the vine for longer, which isn't great for taste or texture—the seeds get bigger and more plentiful, and the skin gets thicker. Look for younger, smaller ones at the market, even if they lack an elegant neck.

Though their shape and color may differ, zucchini and crooknecks taste pretty much the same and are interchangeable in recipes. But at the height of the season, it's worth seeking out other varieties of summer squash: zephyr, with its lime-green bottom half and yellow top; pattypan, the UFO-looking ones with scalloped edges; geode/eight-ball/floridor varieties, which are round; and *costata romanesco*, an Italian type that's sweeter and more flavorful than standard zucchini.

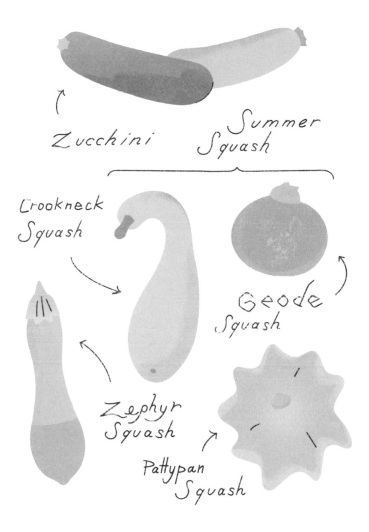

Zucchini

Summer
Squash

Crookneck
Squash

Geode
Squash

Zephyr
Squash

Pattypan
Squash

Cava vs. Champagne vs. Pét-Nat vs. Prosecco

There's nothing quite like a bottle of bubbly to class up any occasion. But you know what makes a situation even classier? Actually knowing what you're drinking.

True **Champagne** can only come from Champagne, France, a region ninety miles northeast of Paris. It's one of the chilliest wine-producing areas in the world and has particularly chalky soil, lending the wine certain characteristics that can't quite be replicated elsewhere.

The process behind Champagne is also unique. All Champagnes are a blend of thirty to sixty separate still wines, which can only be made from three grapes: chardonnay, pinot meunier, and pinot noir. That blend then gets mixed with a bit of reserve wine from earlier years, which gives it more richness and depth. The liquid is combined with a small amount of yeasts and a *liqueur de tirage* (a combination of sugar and wine), then bottled and capped. The yeasts eat the sugar, forming a bit more alcohol and throwing off CO_2, which gets trapped in the bottle and absorbed into the wine. Those bottles rest in a cellar for at least a year, but they're not quite ready yet—there's still the issue of the spent yeast, which makes the mixture cloudy. To get the gunk out, the bottles go through a process that freezes the yeast cells at the very top of the neck; the bottles are then opened, the frozen yeast shoots out, and the resulting 1/4 inch of space is filled with a *liqueur d'expedition* (a combination of wine and sugar) which determines how sweet or dry the Champagne will be. The bottles are then corked until you pop it open, when that trapped carbon dioxide explodes into tiny, fuzzy bubbles.

In the 1860s, a Spanish wine guy named Don José Raventós traveled to Champagne, was super impressed, and started making his own bubbly at home. He and a bunch of nearby winemaking families got together and decided to convert all of the local wines into sparklers, establishing Penedès, where they all lived, as Spain's own Champagne region. Now, their **cava** can legally be made in six regions, but 95 percent of the production is still in Penedès.

Cava must be made with the same dual-fermentation process as Champagne, but it's far from a copycat. The difference in grapes—the five varietals allowed in cava are parellada, xarel-lo, macabeo, chardonnay, and malvasia—and terroir give the wines their own distinct flavors. What's more, most cava is aged for nine months, while many Champagnes are aged at least fifteen months and often much longer. The result is fruitier, brighter, and more citrusy than the French stuff.

Prosecco is from the Veneto region of Italy and is made primarily from Glera (formerly known as prosecco) grapes. It gets its sparkle not through the Champagne method, but the Charmat method: the second fermentation is done in a pressurized tank rather than in each individual bottle. The resulting product is fruitier and less "dramatically crisp" than Champagne, to borrow the words of the *Wine Bible* author Karen MacNeil, with bubbles that are larger and clunkier. No matter—it's an easy-drinking, more affordable option, one that can be consumed with gusto without breaking the bank.

Then there's **pét-nat**, or pétillant naturel, the hippy of the group. Unlike Champagne, cava, and prosecco, which all go through a second fermentation, pét-nat is bottled before the *first* fermentation is complete. The method is simple and rustic and involves a lot of unpredictability, so making a good pét-nat requires a skilled winemaker who can wrangle those what-ifs into something delicious.

There's also the topic of cloudiness. For pét-nats, there's no requirement to remove the spent yeast left over from fermentation—which means some will still have some sediment in the final product. (Some winemakers even prefer it that way.) The method also produces calmer, bigger bubbles, so you'll get more of a laid-back, muted fizz with a vivacity that differs from bottle to bottle.

Since it requires no expensive equipment and isn't bound by region or grape, pét-nat has become a style that any willing producer can try their hand at. That's good news for us drinkers: you get the fun of opening a bottle of bubbly on any random night, and a chance to explore one of the quirkier products the wine world has to offer.

Port, Madeira, and sherry are all fortified wines: wines with the extra *oomph* of a distilled spirit added into the mix, upping the alcohol content and making the resulting liquid more stable. All three of the fortified wines in question are punched up with brandy (page 16).

Port comes from the Douro Valley in Portugal, and the wine used in it must be made with one of the eighty-plus grape varietals in the region. Before the wine is finished fermenting, unaged brandy is mixed in, stopping the process before all the sugars are gobbled up. The result: a sweet, richly flavored concoction that's a great after-dinner sipper.

There are four major styles of port. Vintage, the most expensive, must be made from grapes from a single year and only a year that's declared "worthy" by Portugal's Port Wine Institute. It's always bottled within two years, and the best versions can age at least fifty years. Tawny port is made of a blend of grapes from different years and can be aged in wood for as long as four decades. Its time in the barrel makes for a nutty, oxidized product. Ruby port, which is bright red, is made from lower-quality wine; it's aged in wood for two years and bottled while it's still fruity. White port is made from white grapes and can be drier than the others; the drier the port is, the longer it was allowed to ferment.

Madeira comes from Portugal's Madeira islands, which in the age of exploration were the last stop for ships coming from Europe into the "new world." Wine made on the islands would be stored in large casks and loaded onto the ships for the journey, but there was a problem: wine spoils easily, especially when it's getting sloshed around in permeable wood barrels. So producers borrowed a trick from their friends in the Douro Valley and started mixing in brandy, which prevented the wine from going bad. People started realizing that the heat, movement, and oxygen actually made the product *better*. But loading up ships for the sole purpose of aging wine became too expensive, so producers figured out how to mimic the sea voyage by letting barrels of it bake in the sun or in a hot attic for a while. The result: a wine that was pretty much indestructible, one that people could stock up on without worrying it would spoil and could survive the long trek to the Americas.

Madeira is available in sweet and dry styles; for sweet, unaged brandy is added during the fermentation process, and for dry, it's added afterwards. Malmsey, a particularly sweet, rich variety, is the only type still aged in the sun—the others are now heated in stoves. Madeiras like malmsey are great with dessert, while lighter ones make for great aperitifs.

Sherry comes not from Portugal but from Spain, specifically from three towns in the Andalusia region—though it's now made around the world. It ranges from dry to sweet depending on the type of wine used, where it was made, and how long it was aged. While the wine for sherry ferments, a layer of yeast called "flor" forms on its surface, protecting it from spoiling and giving it a distinctly nutty flavor. When fermentation is complete, the wine is fortified with high-proof brandy and shuttled into barrels. It's then aged using the solera system: barrels of older wine are topped off with younger wine, making the product consistent from year to year.

Fino, amontillado, and oloroso are three of the more famous styles of sherry. Fino spends its whole life under a layer of flor; the result is very delicate and dry and has a distinct salinity.

When the flor blanket doesn't hold, you get amontillado sherry, which gets its darker color and richer, nuttier flavor from being exposed to the air inside the barrels. To make oloroso sherry, the flor blanket is intentionally broken up to promote oxidation, and the product is aged longer than fino or amontillado. The result is a sweeter, darker product that's usually more expensive and consumed at room temperature rather than chilled.

Natural vs. Organic Wine

Natural wine is more of a vibe, a concept, a framework rather than a strictly regulated category. In the most basic sense, it's pure, unadulterated fermented grape juice—the kind of stuff people have been making for millennia. In 2021, what this actually means is

1. the grapes aren't sprayed with pesticides,

2. they're hand-picked instead of harvested by machine,

3. they're fermented only with natural yeast, the stuff hanging out in the air that ends up sticking to them as they hang out in their vat, and

4. they're free of the additives used in the conventional wine-making process, such as sugar, acid, and egg whites (ew).

A hot-button issue in the natural-wine world is that of sulfites, which are preservative chemicals that help kill off natural yeasts and ensure that the product that goes into the bottles tastes like the stuff that comes out of it. Some natural winemakers won't add any sulfites; others will add a little before bottling. In most circles, around 10 to 35 parts per million of added sulfites is considered an acceptable amount. (For scale, conventional winemakers use up to ten times as much.)

In the U.S., **"organic wine"** means that the grapes have been grown without the use of synthetic pesticides and fertilizers and that all of the ingredients, including the yeast, are certified organic. The only sulfites allowed are the ones that occur naturally. In the E.U., however, organic wines can contain up to 100 parts per million of sulfites—one of the very few instances in which the U.S. has higher standards of quality than Europe.

Shoutouts

A special shoutout to everyone who suggested ideas over the years that ended up in this book: Sabas Abuabara, Bree Arditi, Suzy Bell, Jenna Berger, Marian Bull, Hannah Clark, Michelle Curb, John deBary, Ari Dwyer, Max Falkowitz, Ben Fleischman, Lisa Gabor, Jordan Zarrilli Green, Ross Green, Jake Greenberg, Sam Greenberg, Michael Hoffman, Michael Ira, Sarah Jampel, Pamela Sheldon Johns, Arielle Johnson, Karen Koeppel, Ben Leffell, Alli Letica-Kriegel, Nick Letica, Peggy Loftus, Helen Maxman, Kylie Foxx McDonald, Ezra Mechaber, Jared Moscow, Hyland Murphy, David Plotz, Alex Rivkin, Ben Ross, Alex Sater, Amanda Shulman, Jessica Skipper, Lily Starbuck, Evie Stroup, Sarit Tolzis, Jeff Warshaw, Sammy Warshaw, Sheri Warshaw, Vivien Yip, and Julie Zuckerbrod.

Acknowledgments

This book would not exist without the amazing subscribers to the *What's the Difference?* newsletter. Thank you for reading, for suggesting ideas, and for staying so enthusiastic and engaged all these years. Many thanks to Kim Witherspoon, Karen Rinaldi, and Rebecca Raskin for turning this weird idea into the book you're holding in your hands; to Sophia Foster-Dimino for bringing these words to life; to Erin McDowell, Jim Meehan, Justin Kennedy, and the various other experts who let me absorb their wisdom; to my colleagues at Apple, especially Kate Stroup, Maggie Day Brito, and Ruth Spencer, for making me a better writer and editor every day; to my dear friends—including but not limited to Bree Arditi, Jenna Berger, Marian Bull, Jena Derman, Jordan Zarrilli Green, Michael Ira, Alli Letica-Kriegel, and Rebecca Palkovics—for keeping me sane throughout this process; to my late, great friend Jason Polan, who was a fervent champion of *WTD*; to the Greencow crew—Karen, Ed, Jake, Sam, Stevie, Casey, and Drew—for welcoming me into their clan as I toiled away on this book; to my loving, fantastic, one-of-a-kind family for their unwavering enthusiasm; and to Jared, for giving me the strength and support to make this book happen.

Selected Bibliography

Beranbaum, Rose Levy. "The Best Flour for Baking Bread—and How to Use It."
    Epicurious, August 31, 2016, https://www.epicurious
    .com/expert-advice/bread-ingredients-guide-to-flours-for
    -homemade-dough-article.

Beranbaum, Rose Levy. *The Baking Bible.* New York: Houghton Mifflin
    Harcourt, 2014.

Bittman, Mark. *How to Bake Everything: Simple Recipes for the Best Baking.*
    New York: Houghton Mifflin Harcourt, 2016.

Boone, Rhoda. "Bone Broth vs. Stock: What's the Difference?" Epicurious,
    December 7, 2017, https://www.epicurious.com
    /ingredients/difference-stock-broth-bone-broth-article.

Bousel, Joshua. "Mustard Manual: Your Guide to Mustard Varieties." Serious
    Eats, August 10, 2018, https://www.seriouseats
    .com/2014/05/mustard-manual-guide-different-types-mustard
    varieties-dijon-brown-spicy-yellow-hot-whole-grain.html.

*The Cook's Illustrated Meat Book: The Game-Changing Guide That Teaches
    You How to Cook Meat and Poultry with 425 Bulletproof Recipes.* Brookline,
    MA: America's Test Kitchen, 2014.

Dean, Sam. "The Origin of Hoagies, Grinders, Subs, Heroes, and Spuckies."
    Bon Appétit, February 1, 2013, https://www.bonappetit
    .com/test-kitchen/ingredients/article/the-origin-of-hoagies-grinders-
    subs-heroes-and-spuckies.

DeMichele, Kristina. "Different Types of Chocolate and How to Use Them."
    Cook's Illustrated, October 26, 2018, https://www
    .cooksillustrated.com/articles/1333-all-about-the-different-types
    -of-chocolate-and-how-to-use-them.

"Dinner vs. Supper: Is There a Difference?" Merriam-Webster, accessed July
    23, 2020, https://www.merriam-webster.com/words
    -at-play/dinner-vs-supper-difference-history-meaning.

Draoulec, Pascale Le. "Who's Who in the Dining Room." *Los Angeles Times,*
    October 24, 2007, https://www.latimes.com/archives
    /la-xpm-2007-oct-24-fo-serviceside24-story.html.

Falkowitz, Max. "Is Aioli Really Just Mayonnaise?" TASTE, January 30, 2020,
    https://www.tastecooking.com/aioli-really-just
    -mayonnaise/.

Finger, Bobby. "Is Cold Brew Better Than Iced Coffee?" *New York Times,* July
    2, 2019, https://www.nytimes.com/2019/07/02/style
    /self-care/cold-brew-iced-coffee-difference.html.

Foster, Kelli. "What's the Difference Between Broccoli, Broccolini, Broccoli
    Rabe, and Chinese Broccoli?" The Kitchn, January 7, 2016, https://www.
    thekitchn.com/whats-the-difference-between
    -broccoli-broccolini-broccoli-rabe-and-chinese-broccoli-227025.

Goldwyn, Meathead. "Barbecue History." BBQ & Grilling In Depth: Up Your Game with Tested Recipes, Science-Based Tips on Technique, Equipment Reviews, Community, June 21, 2020, https://amazingribs.com/barbecue-history-and-culture/barbecue-history.

Goldwyn, Meathead. "Benchmark Barbecue Sauces and How to Make Them." BBQ & Grilling In Depth: Up Your Game with Tested Recipes, Science-Based Tips on Technique, Equipment Reviews, Community, December 30, 2019, https://amazingribs.com/tested-recipes/barbecue-sauce-recipes/benchmark-barbecue-sauces-how-make-them-and-how-buy-set-award.

Harbison, Martha. "What Is the Difference between a Lager and an Ale?" *Popular Science*, January 25, 2013, accessed August 12, 2020, https://www.popsci.com/science/article/2013-01/beersci-what-difference-between-lager-and-ale/.

Herbst, Sharon Tyler, and Ron Herbst. *The New Food Lover's Companion.* Hauppage, NY: Barron's Educational Series, Inc., 2013.

Hildebrand, Caz, and Jacob Kenedy. *The Geometry of Pasta.* Philadelphia, PA: Quirk Books, 2010.

Jampel, Sarah. "Light Versus Dark Brown Sugar: What's the Deal?" *Bon Appétit*, May 28, 2020, https://www.bonappetit.com/story/light-versus-dark-brown-sugar.

Jampel, Sarah. "There Are 40,000 Types of Rice in the World—Here's How to Pick the One You Need." *Bon Appétit*, January 21, 2020, https://www.bonappetit.com/story/types-of-rice.

Jenkins, Nancy Harmon. "The Deep-Fried Truth About Ipswich Clams; No Matter the Source of the Harvest, the Secret to a Classic Seaside Meal May Be the Mud." *New York Times*, August 21, 2002, https://www.nytimes.com/2002/08/21/dining/deep-fried-truth-about-ipswich-clams-no-matter-source-harvest-secret-classic.html.

Joachim, David and Andrew Schloss. "The Science of Caramel." *Fine Cooking*, August 22, 2014, https://www.finecooking.com/article/the-science-of-caramel.

Khong, Rachel. *All About Eggs: Everything We Know About the World's Most Important Food.* New York: Clarkson Potter, 2017.

Mancall-Bitel, Nicholas. "What Is Peat, Anyway?" Thrillist, October 7, 2016, https://www.thrillist.com/culture/what-is-peat-and-what-does-it-have-to-do-with-whisky.

McGee, Harold. *McGee on Food & Cooking: An Encyclopedia of Kitchen Science, History and Culture.* London, UK: Hodder & Stoughton, 2004.

McKenna, Amy. "What's the Difference between Whiskey and Whisky? What About Scotch, Bourbon, and Rye?" Encyclopædia Britannica, accessed July 21, 2020, https://www.britannica.com/story/whats-the-difference-between-whiskey-and-whisky-what-about-scotch-bourbon-and-rye.

Meehan, Jim. *Meehan's Bartender Manual.* Berkeley, CA: Ten Speed Press, 2017.

Meister, Erin. "Coffee Drinks: A Visual Glossary." Serious Eats, accessed July 22, 2020, https://drinks.seriouseats.com/2012/06

/coffee-comparison-a-visual-glossary-of-some-common-drinks
-slideshow.html.

Morthland, John. "A Plague of Pigs in Texas." Smithsonian.com, January 1,
2011, https://www.smithsonianmag.com/science
-nature/a-plague-of-pigs-in-texas-73769069/.

Moskin, Julia. "Basic Knife Skills." *New York Times*, accessed July 23, 2020,
https://cooking.nytimes.com/guides/23-basic-knife-skills.

Mulvany, Lydia. "The Parmesan Cheese You Sprinkle on Your Penne Could Be
Wood." Bloomberg, February 16, 2016, https://www
.bloomberg.com/news/articles/2016-02-16/the-parmesan-cheese
-you-sprinkle-on-your-penne-could-be-wood?srcf=rsBIQ6iD.

Nosrat, Samin. *Salt, Fat, Acid, Heat: Mastering the Elements of Good Cooking.*
New York: Simon & Schuster, 2017.

Parks, Stella. "Skip Dulce de Leche: Cajeta Is All You Need." Serious Eats,
February 5, 2019, https://www.seriouseats.com/2016/04
/how-to-make-goats-milk-cajeta.html.

Parsons, Russ. "Aspiration: Asparation." *Los Angeles Times*, March 18, 1998,
https://www.latimes.com/archives/la-xpm-1998-mar-18-fo
-29958-story.html.

Prakash, Sheela. "How to Make Your Own Superfine, Powdered, and Brown
Sugars." Epicurious, November 2, 2016, https://www
.epicurious.com/expert advice/how-to-make-your-own-superfine
-powdered-and-brown-sugars-article.

Prouse, Margaret. "Understanding Canapés, Hors d'Oeuvres." *Guardian*,
November 30, 2016, https://www.theguardian.pe.ca
/news/provincial/margaret-prouse-understanding canapes hors
-doeuvres-112667/.

Rolland, Jacques L. *The Cook's Essential Kitchen Dictionary: A Complete
Culinary Resource.* Toronto,: Robert Rose Inc., 2014.

Ruggeri, Amanda. "Italy's Practically Perfect Food." BBC, January 28, 2019,
http://www.bbc.com/travel/story/20190127-italys
-practically-perfect-food.

Saffitz, Claire. "Baking Powder vs. Baking Soda: What's the Difference?" *Bon
Appétit*, July 25, 2017, https://www.bonappetit
.com/story/baking-powder-vs-baking-soda-difference.

Samadzadeh, Nozlee. "Down & Dirty: Summer Squash." Food52, August 10,
2012, https://food52.com/blog/4196-down-dirty
-summer-squash.

"Sherbet vs. Sherbert: What's the Scoop?" Merriam-Webster, n.d., https://
www.merriam-webster.com/words-at-play/sherbet-vs
-sherbert.

Teclemariam, Tammie. "What You Need to Know About Cognac vs
Armagnac." *Wine Enthusiast*, October 18, 2019, https://www
.winemag.com/2019/10/17/cognac-armagnac-guide/.

Waters, Alice L. *Chez Panisse Vegetables.* New York: William Morrow
Cookbooks, 2014.

Wilson, Joy. "Baking 101: Natural vs Dutch-Processed Cocoa Powder." *Joy the
Baker*, October 10, 2013, https://joythebaker.com/2013/10

/baking-101-natural-vs-dutch-processed-cocoa-powder/.

Zanini De Vita, Oretta. *Encyclopedia of Pasta.* Translated by Maureen B. Fant. Berkeley: University of California Press, 2009.

Zimberoff, Larissa. "Where to Buy Legal Beluga Caviar in USA: Sturgeon Aquafarms, Huso." Bloomberg, June 26, 2019, https://www.bloomberg.com/news/articles/2019-06-26/where-to-buy-legal-beluga-caviar-in-usa-sturgeon-aquafarms-huso.

Index

About the Author

BRETTE WARSHAW is a writer living in New York City. She's an editor at Apple News and has worked at publications such as *Lucky Peach* and Food52. In her free time, she enjoys throwing dinner parties and organizing her pantry.